Eugene J. Martin's Bamboo Reed Pen and Ink Drawings: 1981–1982

Suzanne Fredericq

ISBN: 978-0-578-02872-9

Eugene James Martin (b. Washington, D.C., July 24, 1938 - d. Lafayette, Louisiana, January 1, 2005) was a prolific African American visual artist.

Eugene J. Martin's art is best known for his imaginative, complex mixed media collages on paper, his often gently humorous pencil and pen and ink drawings, and his paintings on paper and canvas that may incorporate whimsical allusions to animal, machine and structural imagery among areas of "pure", constructed, biomorphic, or disciplined lyrical abstraction.

Eugene Martin's works of art can be found in numerous private art collections throughout the world, and are included in the permanent collection of the Ogden Museum of Southern Art, New Orleans; the Alexandria Museum of Art, Louisiana; the Stowitts Museum & Library in Pacific Grove, California; the Munich Museum of Modern Art; the Arthur Schomburg Center for Research in Black Culture, New York; the Mobile Museum of Art, Alabama; the Walter O. Evans Collection of African American Art in Savannah, Georgia, the Paul R. Jones Collection of African American Art at the University of Delaware, the Walter Anderson Museum of Art in Ocean Springs, Mississippi, and the Louisiana State University Museum of Art in the Shaw Center for the Arts in Baton Rouge, Louisiana.

http://www.artnet.com/awc/eugene-j-martin.html

http://www.artstor.org/what-is-artstor/w-html/col-martin.shtml

http://www.youtube.com/nemastoma

Foreword

This publication includes reproductions of fifty small-sized bamboo reed pen and ink drawings created by visual artist Eugene James Martin (1938-2005) between 1981 and 1982 in Washington D.C.

Suzanne Fredericq,

Lafayette, Louisiana, June 10, 2009

As have the Chinese and English languages,
Eugene has stripped his grammar to the naked bone,
sinewed the simple frame, and created
a rich vocabulary of meaning, sight and emotion.
Yet, always there is discipline.

Thomas Stark

Eugene James Martin, untitled, s.d. (1981), 8.8 x 7"

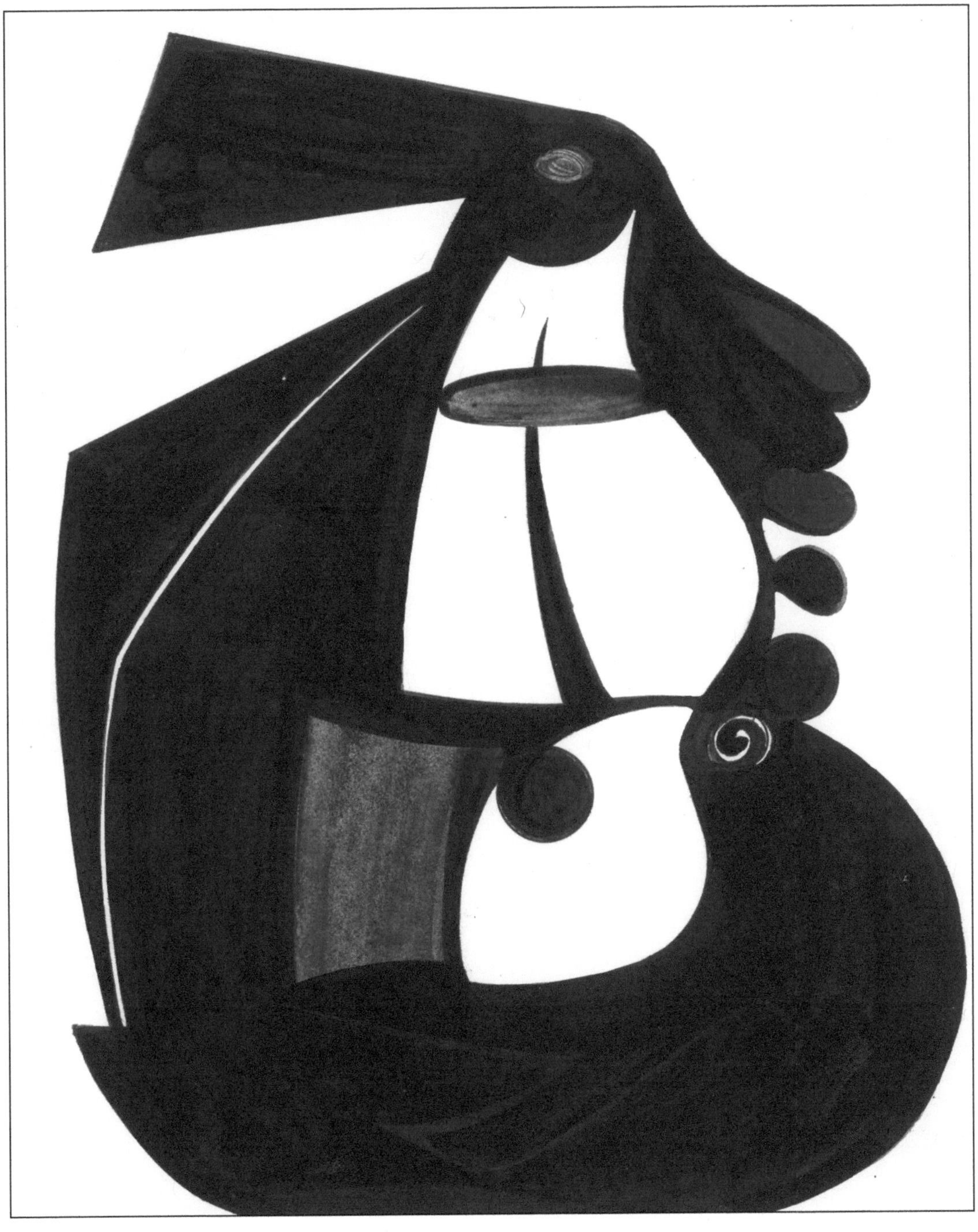

Eugene James Martin, Show-Off II, 1982, 9/5 x 7"

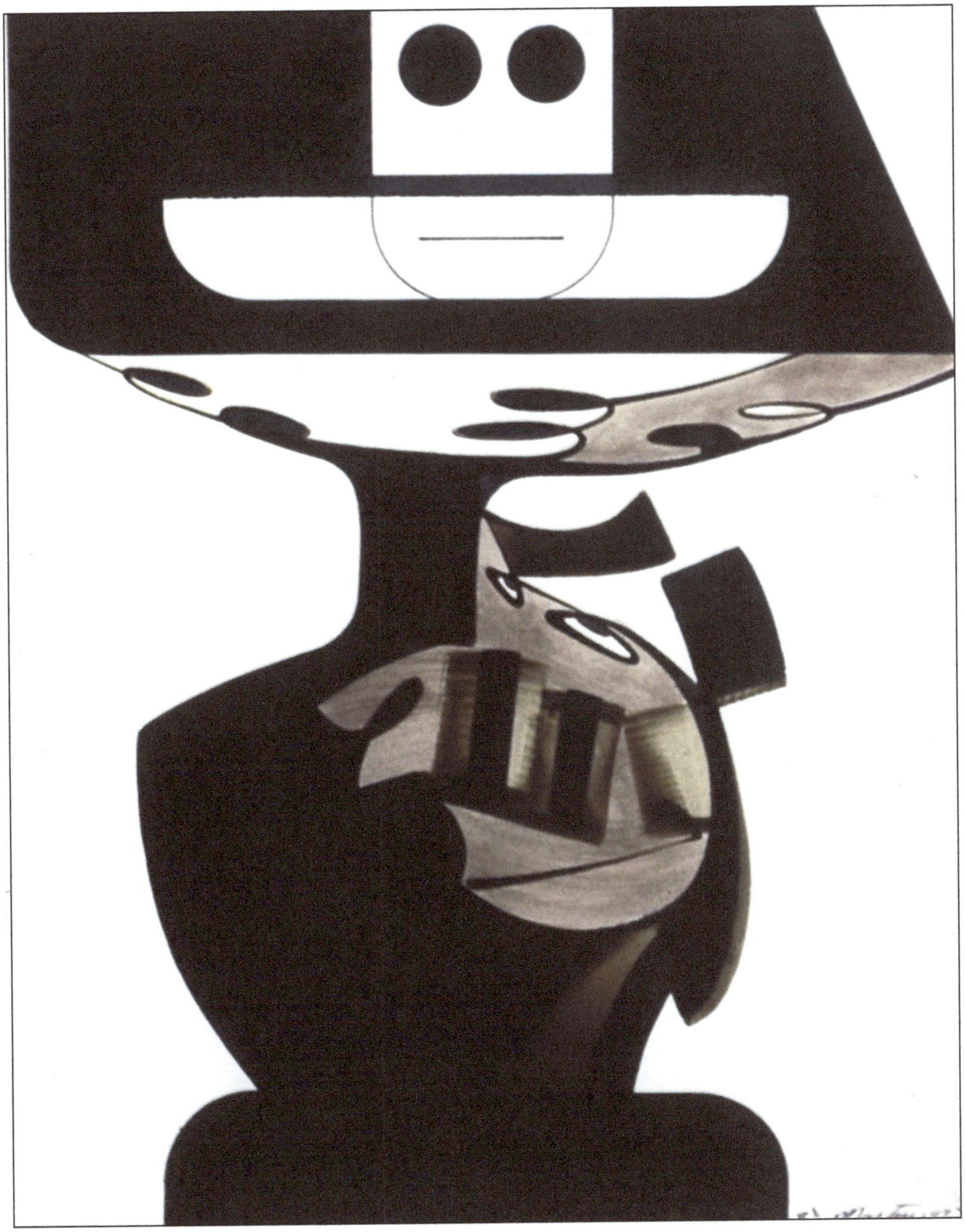

Eugene James Martin, untitled, 1981, 9.5 x 7 "

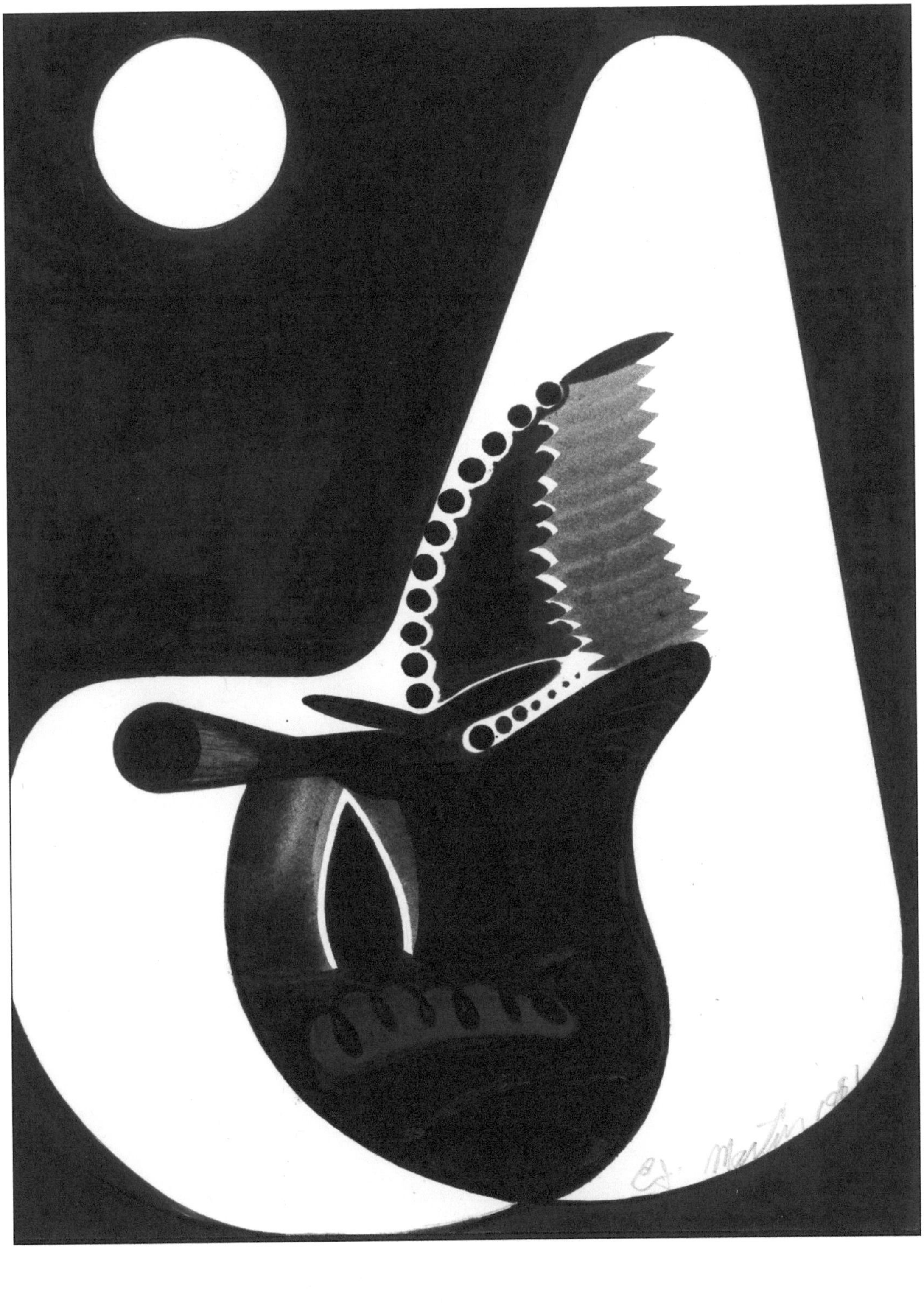

Eugene James Martin, untitled, s.d. (1981), 10 x 7"

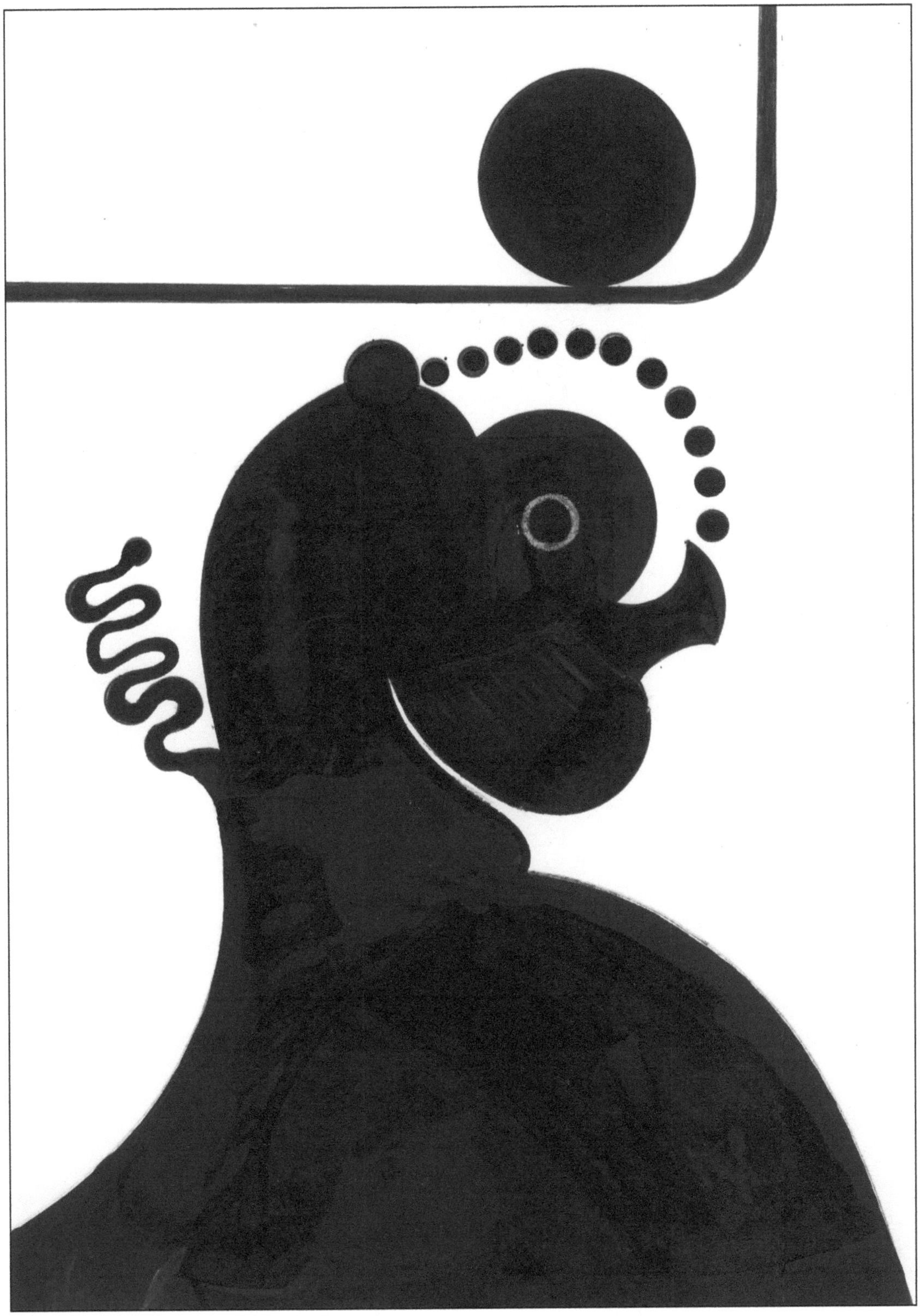

Eugene James Martin, untitled, 1982, 9.5 x 7"

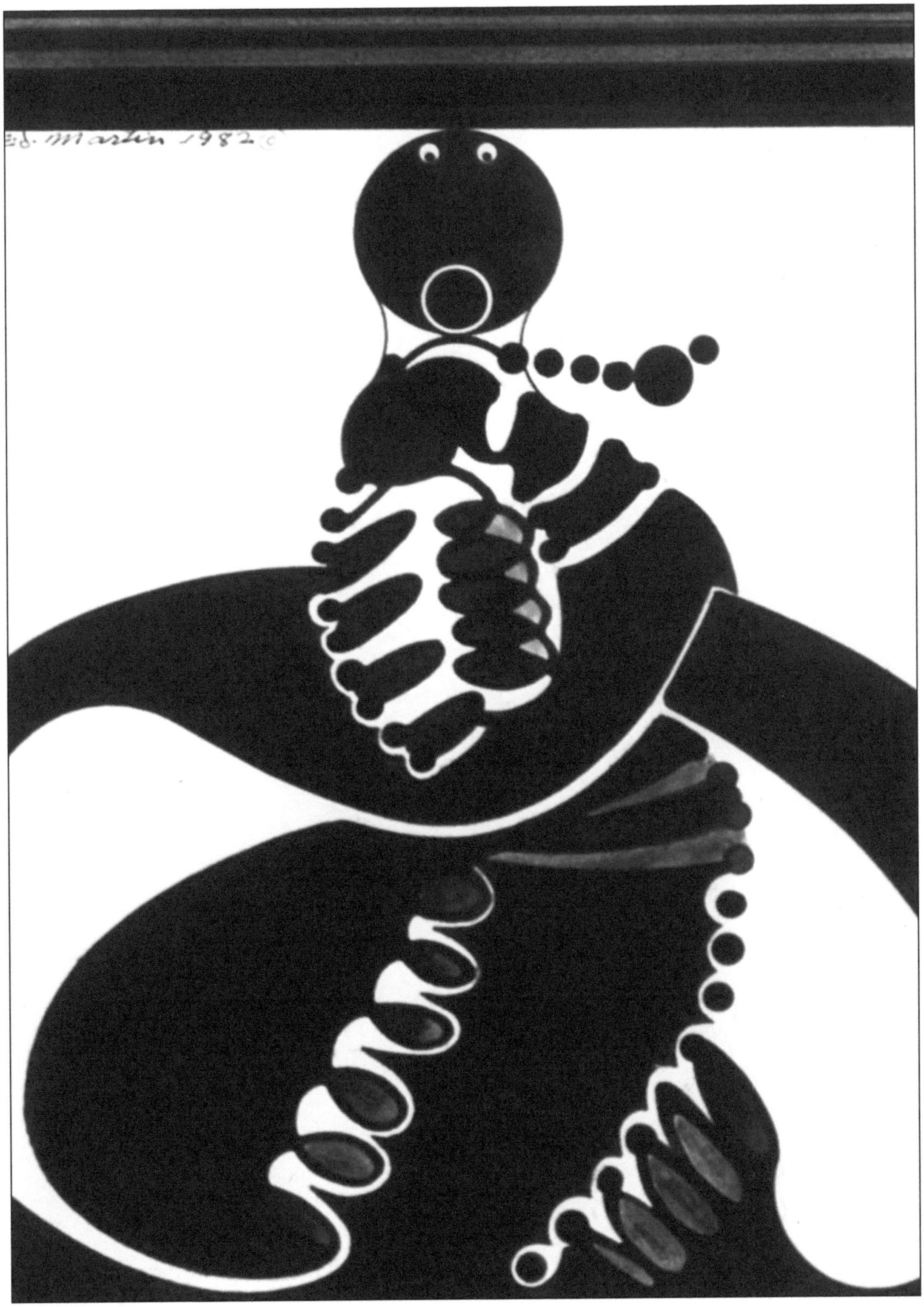

Eugene James Martin, untitled, s.d. (1982), 9.5 x 7"

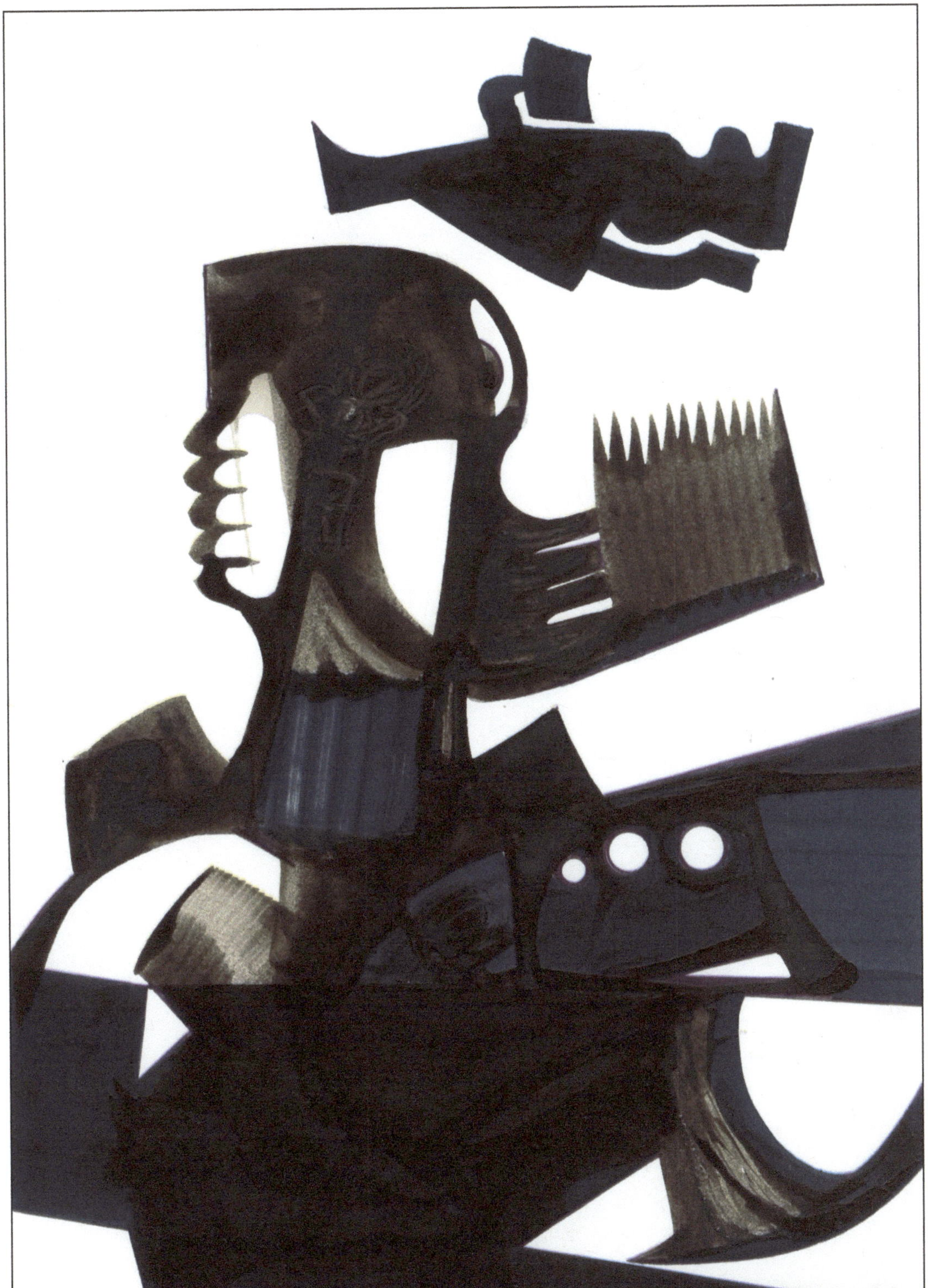

Eugene James Martin, untitled, 1981, 9.5 x 7"

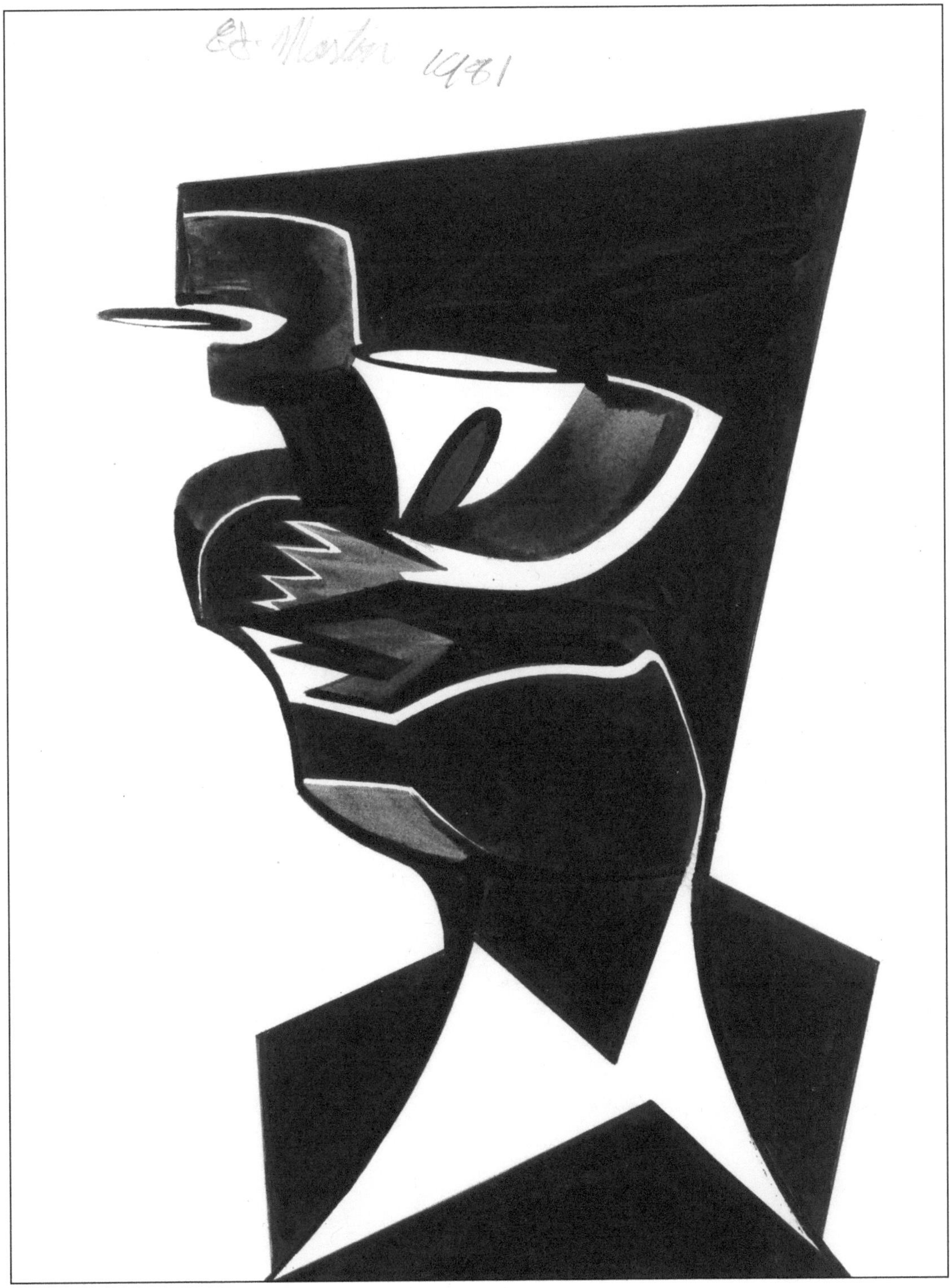

Eugene James Martin, untitled, 1981, 9.5 x 7"

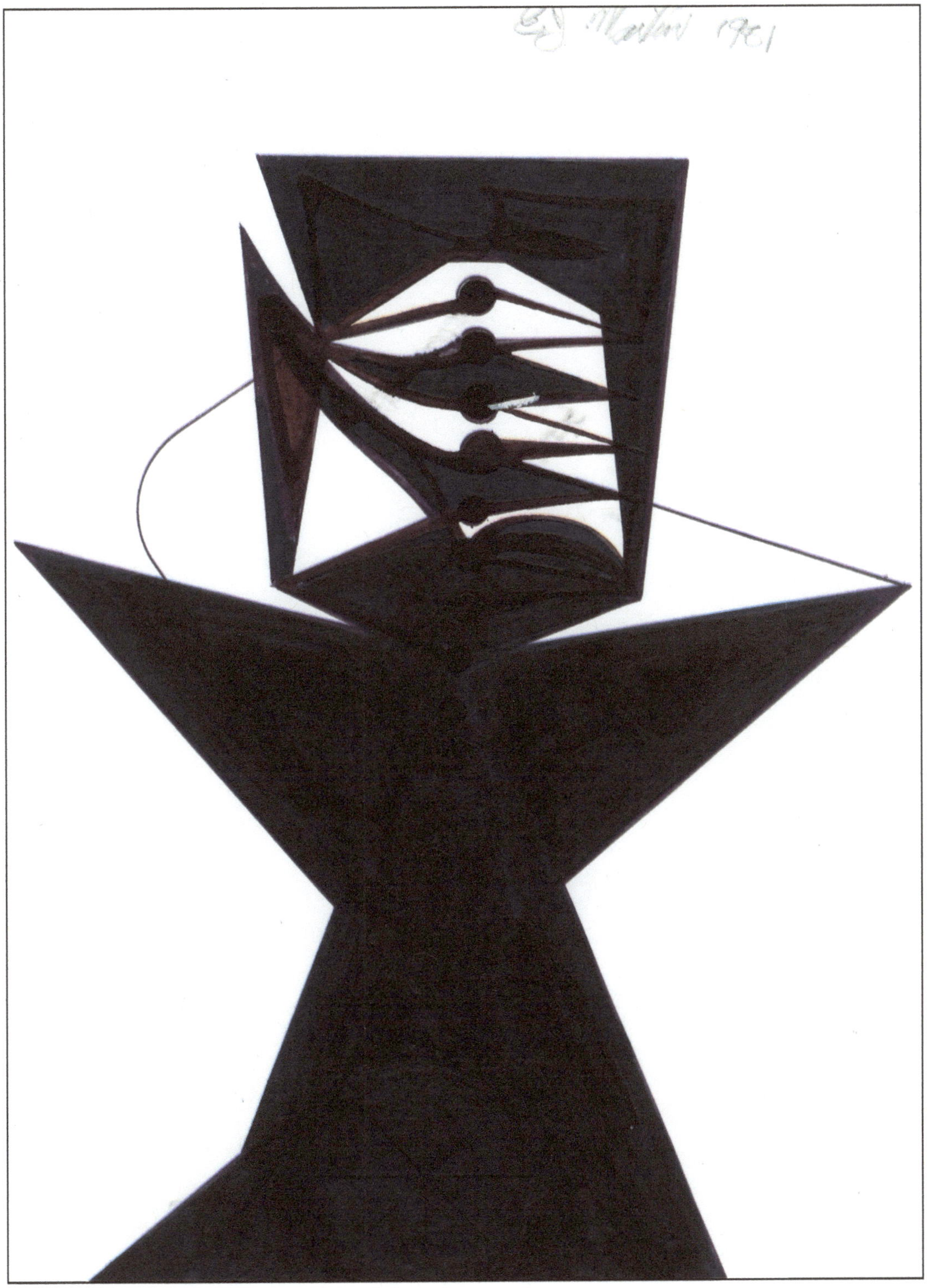

Eugene James Martin, untitled, 1981, 9.8 x 7"

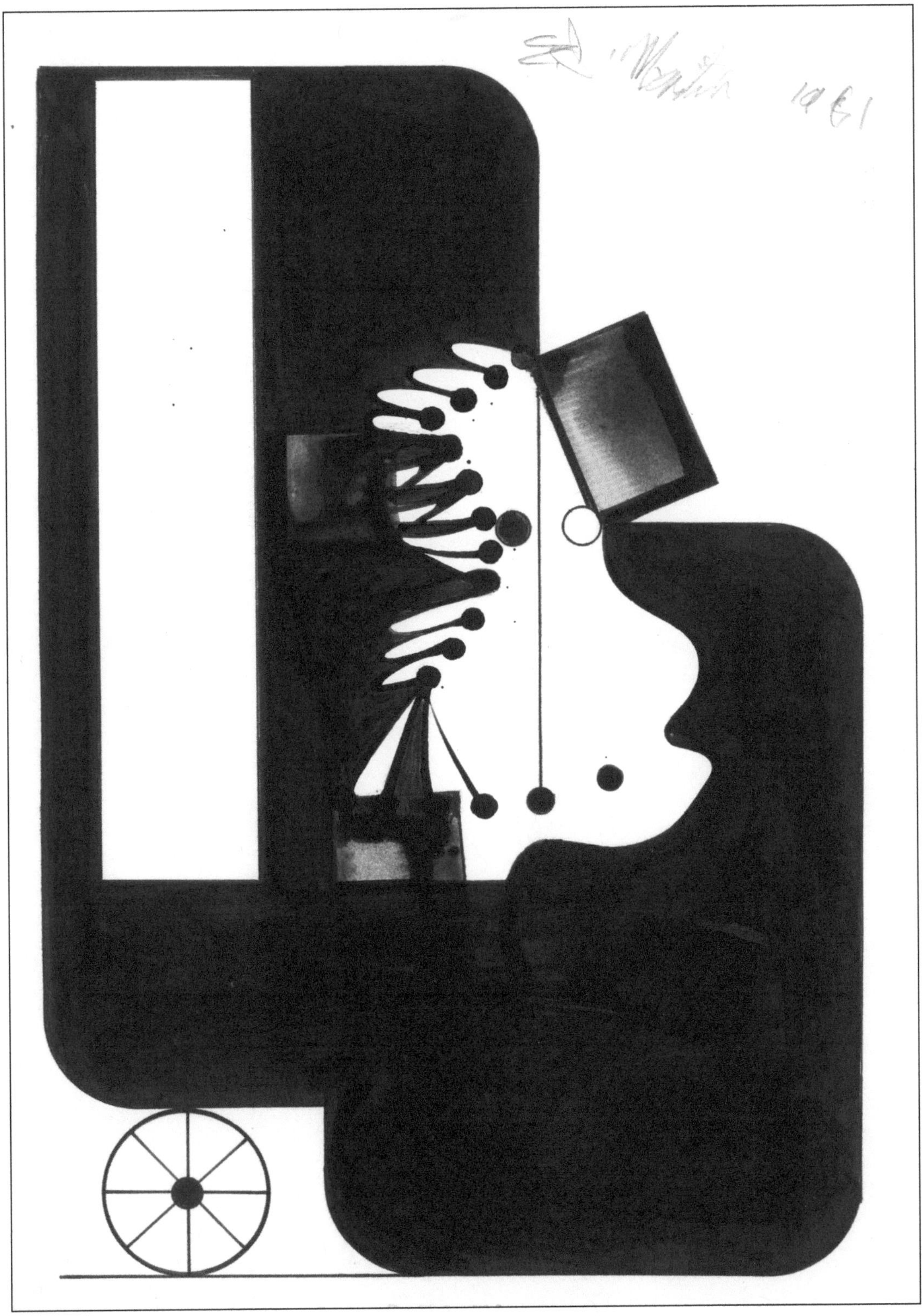

Eugene James Martin, untitled, s.d. (1982), 9.8 x 7"

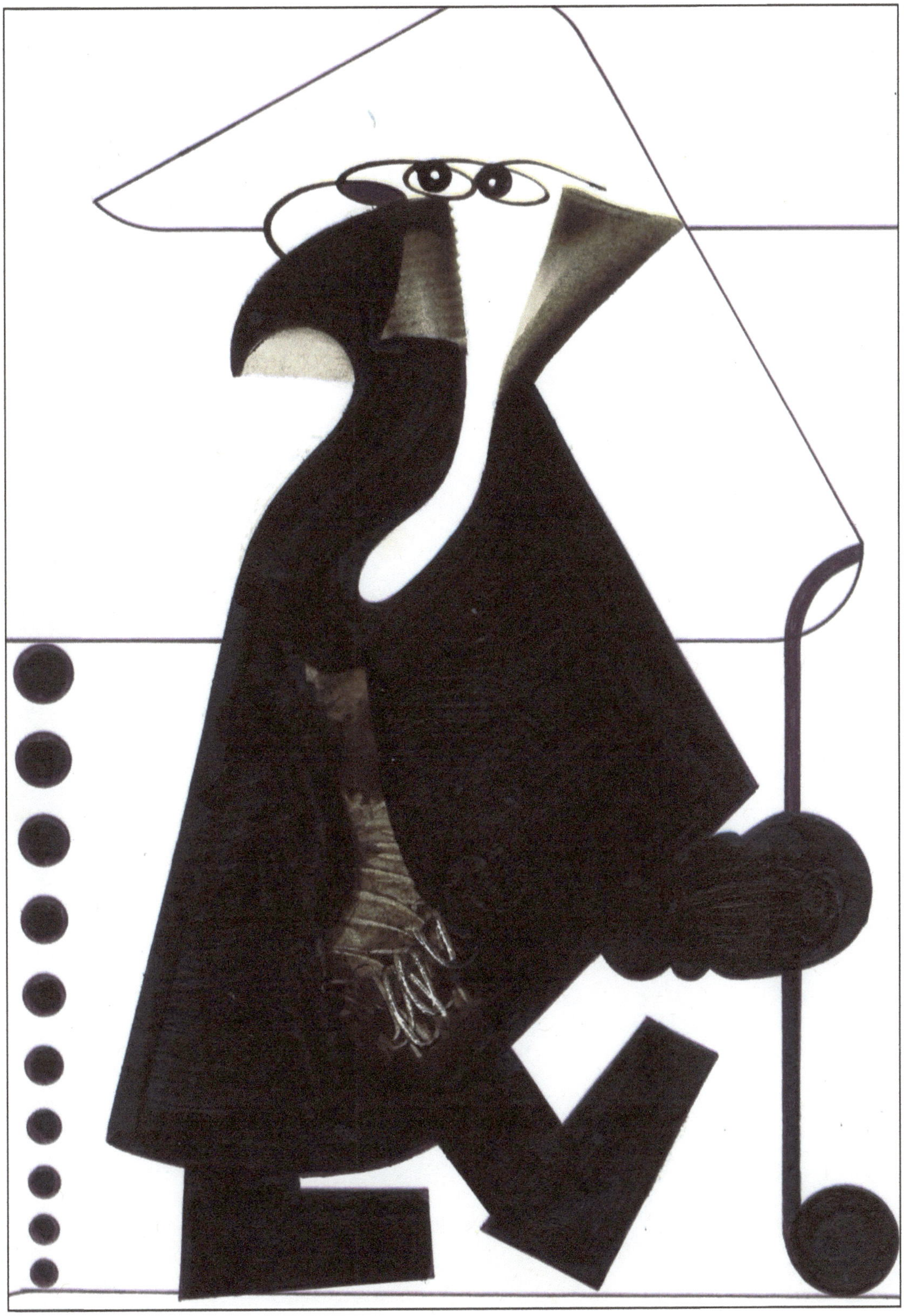

Eugene James Martin, The Music Teacher, 1981, 9 x 6.5"

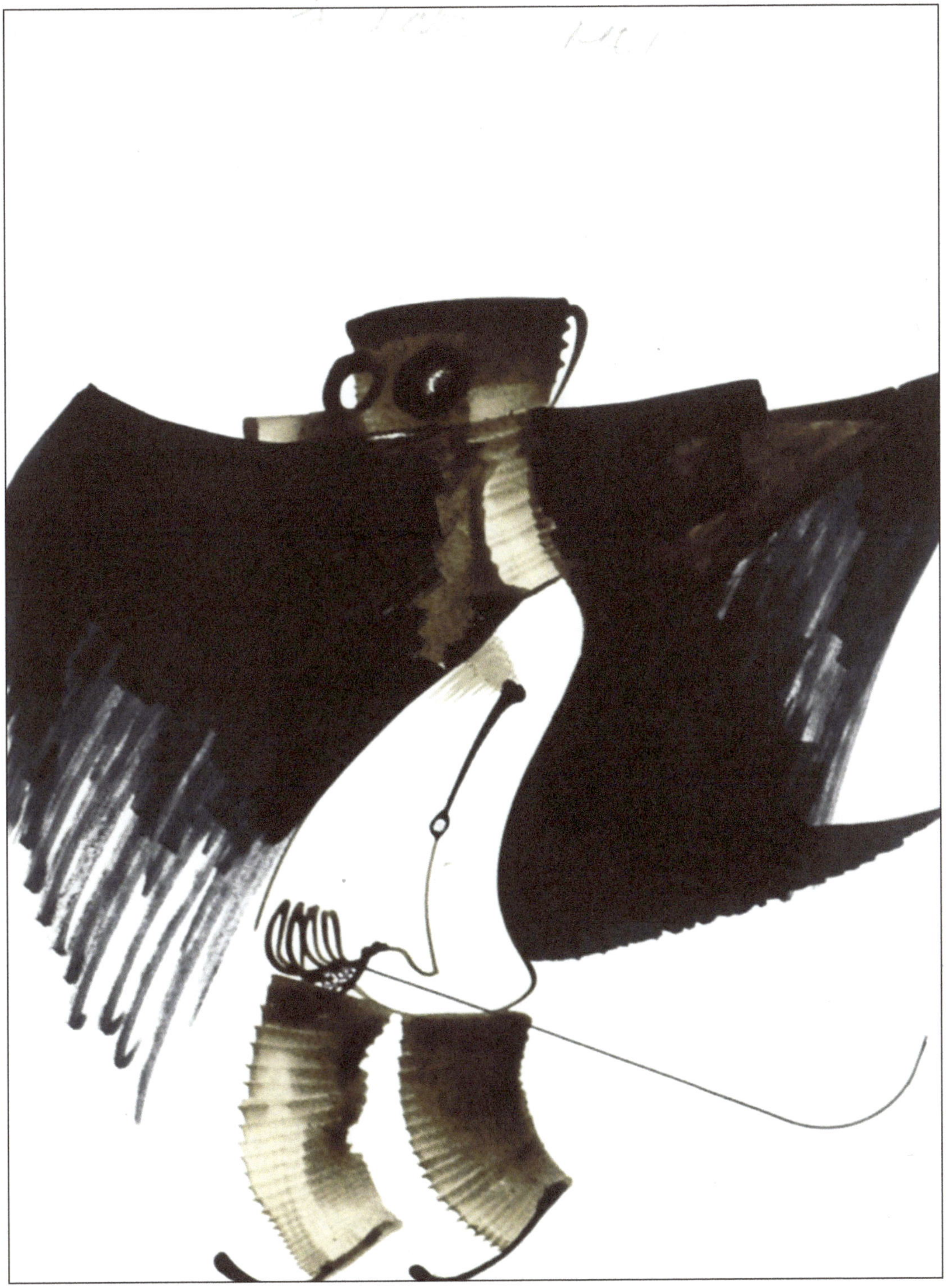

Eugene James Martin, untitled, 1981, 10.2 x 8"

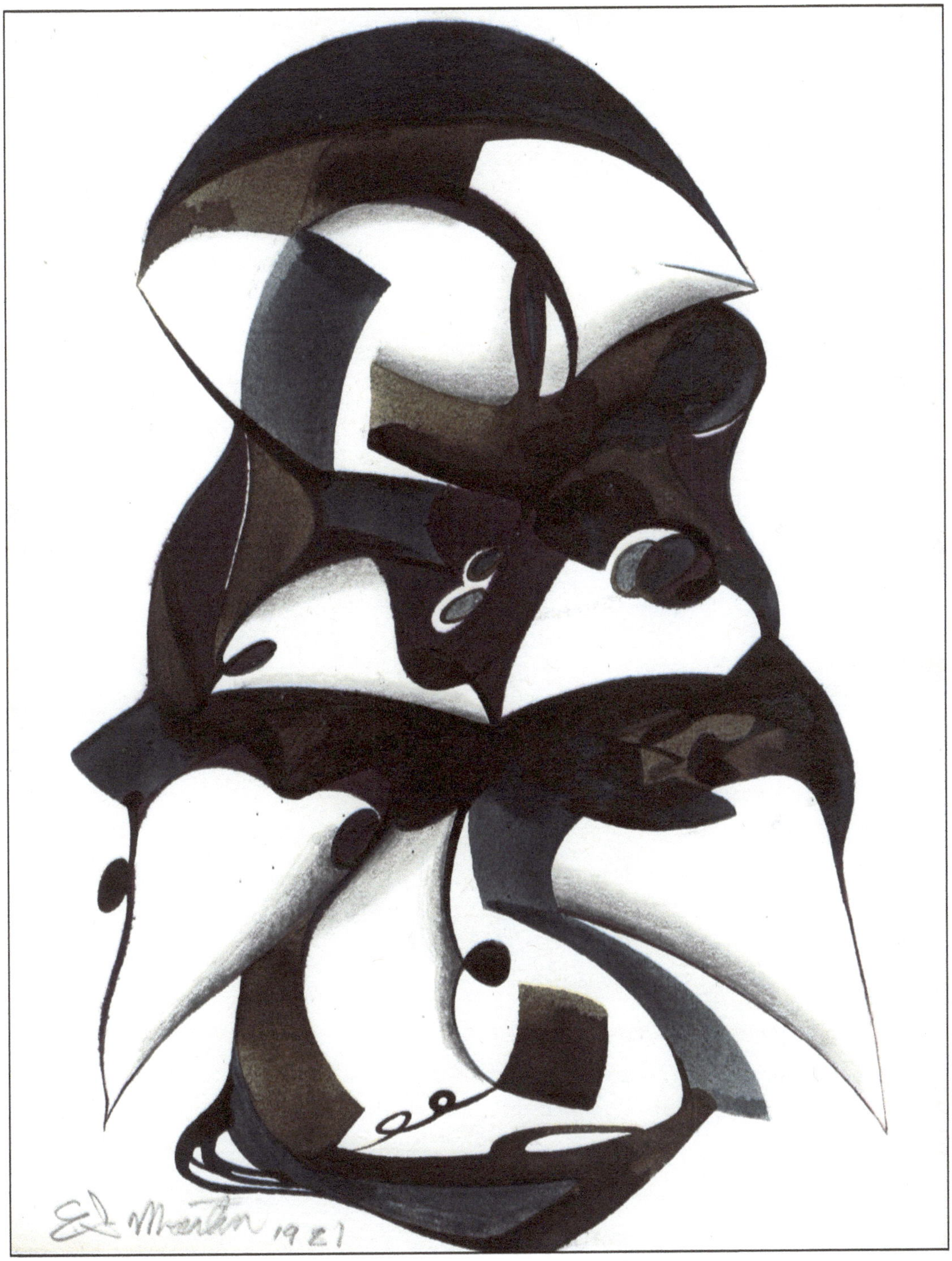

Eugene James Martin, Schizophrenia, 1982, 9 x 7"

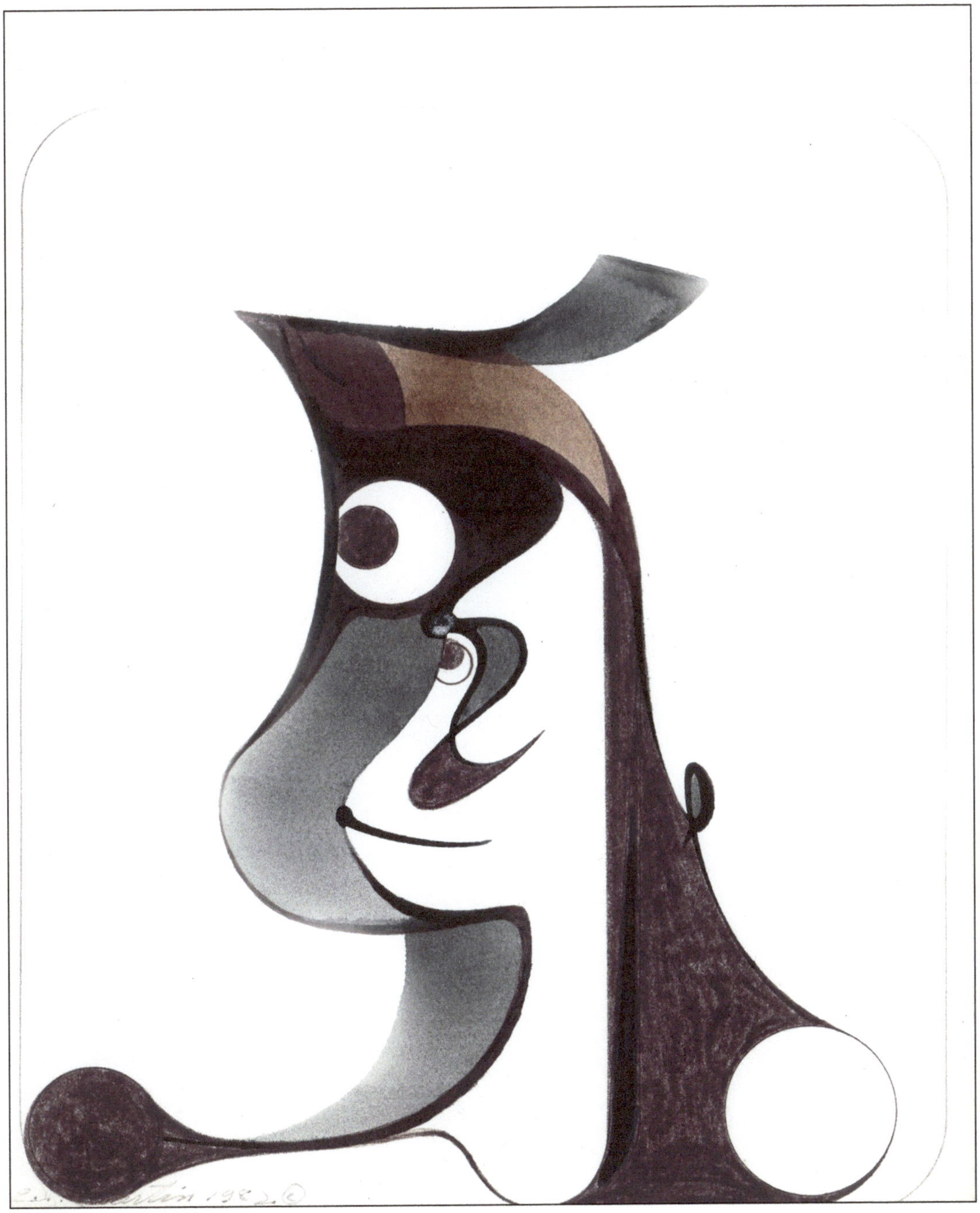

Eugene James Martin, untitled, 1982, 10.5 x 8.2"

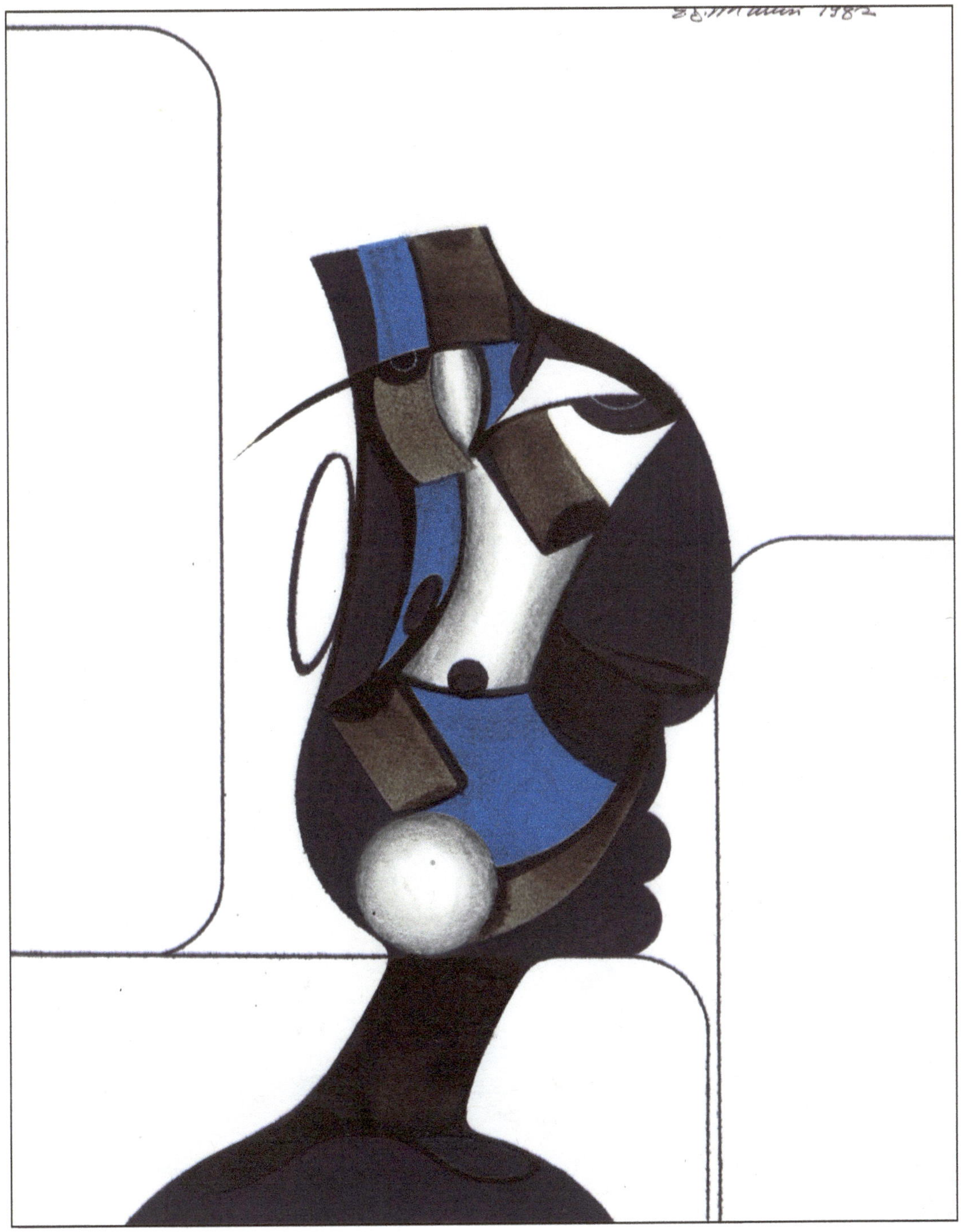

Eugene James Martin, untitled, 1982, 8.5 x 6.2"

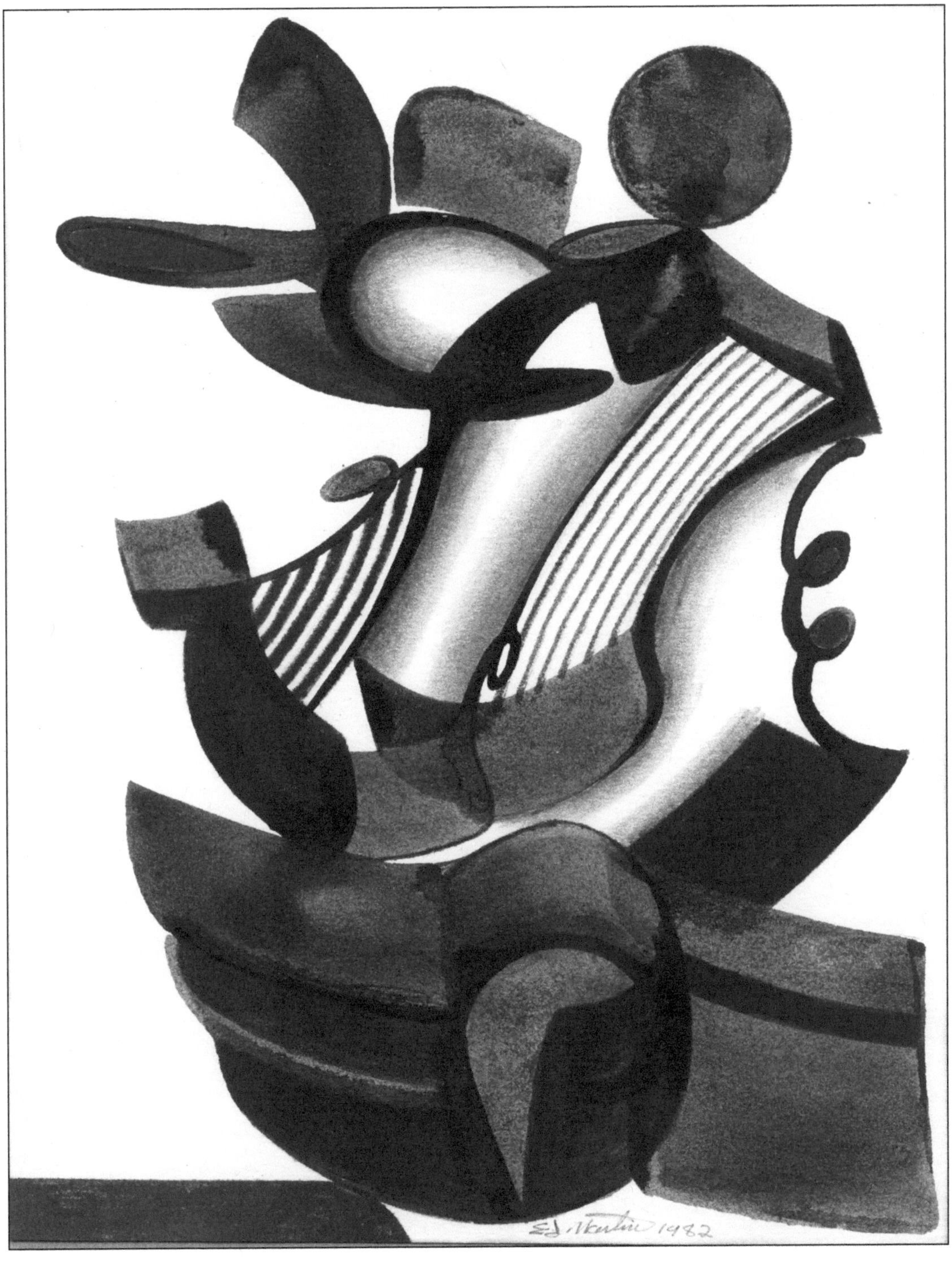

Eugene James Martin, Theatre, 1982, 10.5 x 8.2"

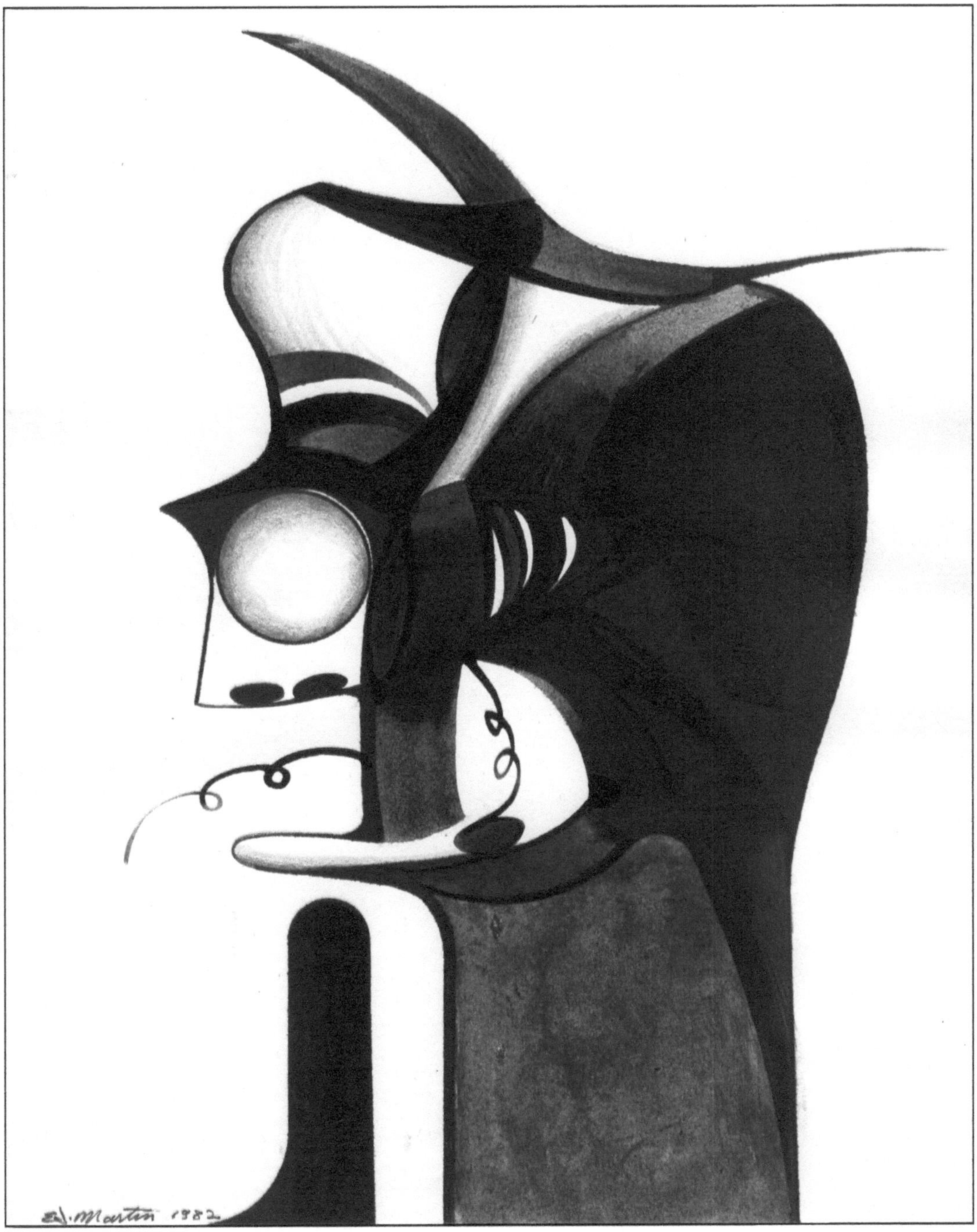
E.J. Martin 1982

Eugene James Martin, untitled, s.d. (1982), 6.8 x 6"

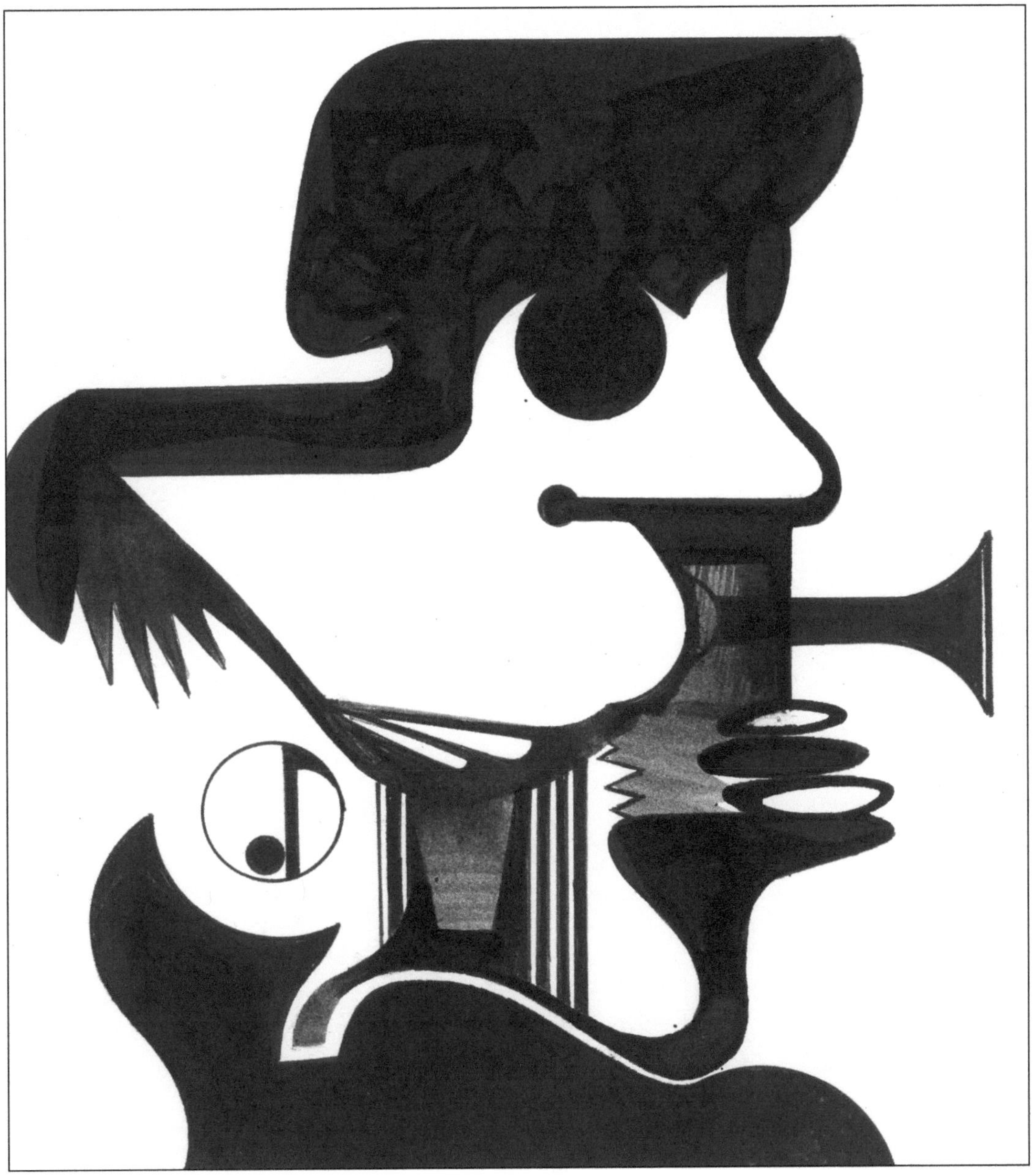

Eugene James Martin, untitled, s.d. (1982), 8.2 x 5"

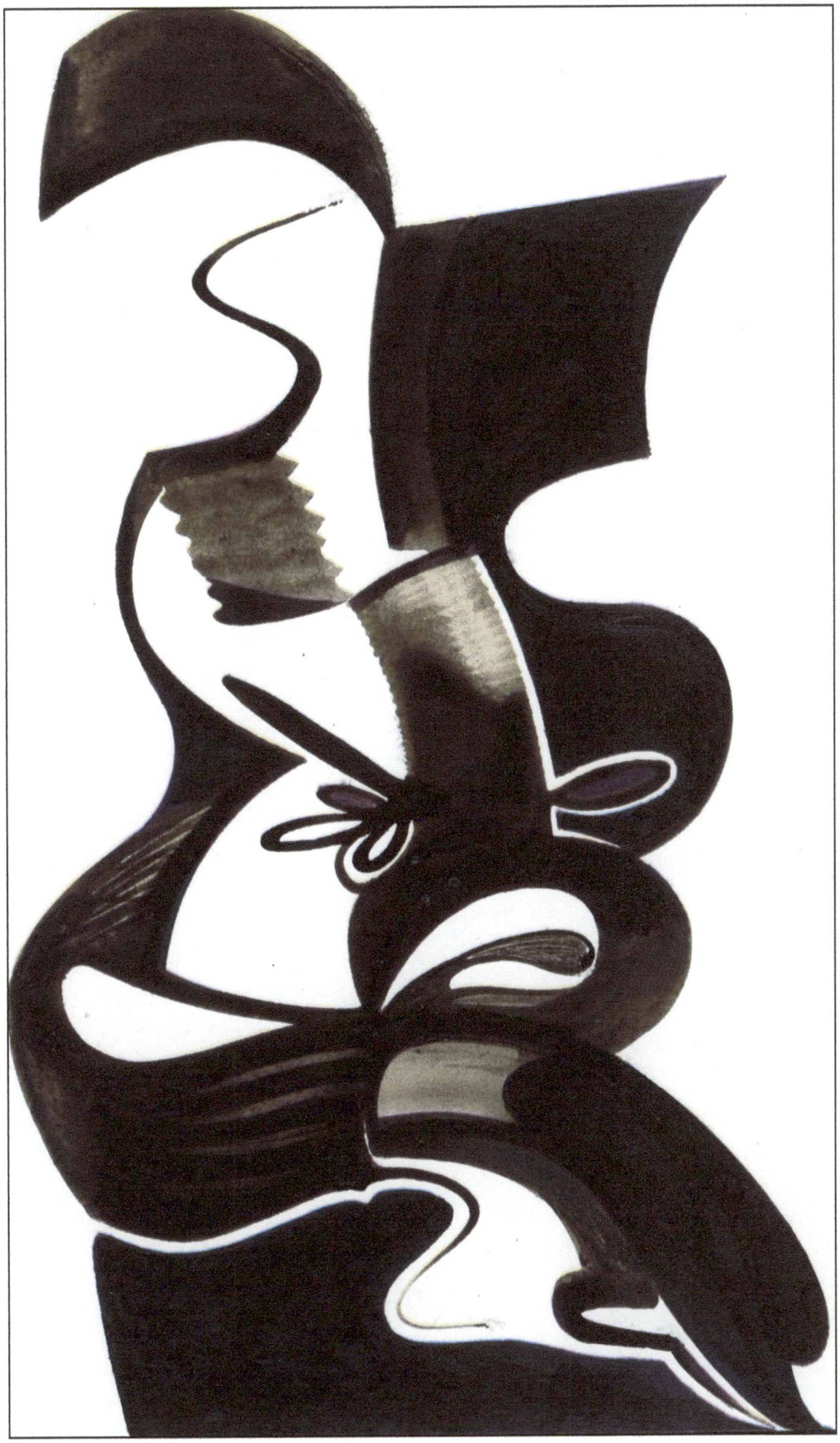

Eugene James Martin, untitled, s.d. (1981), 9.5 x 7"

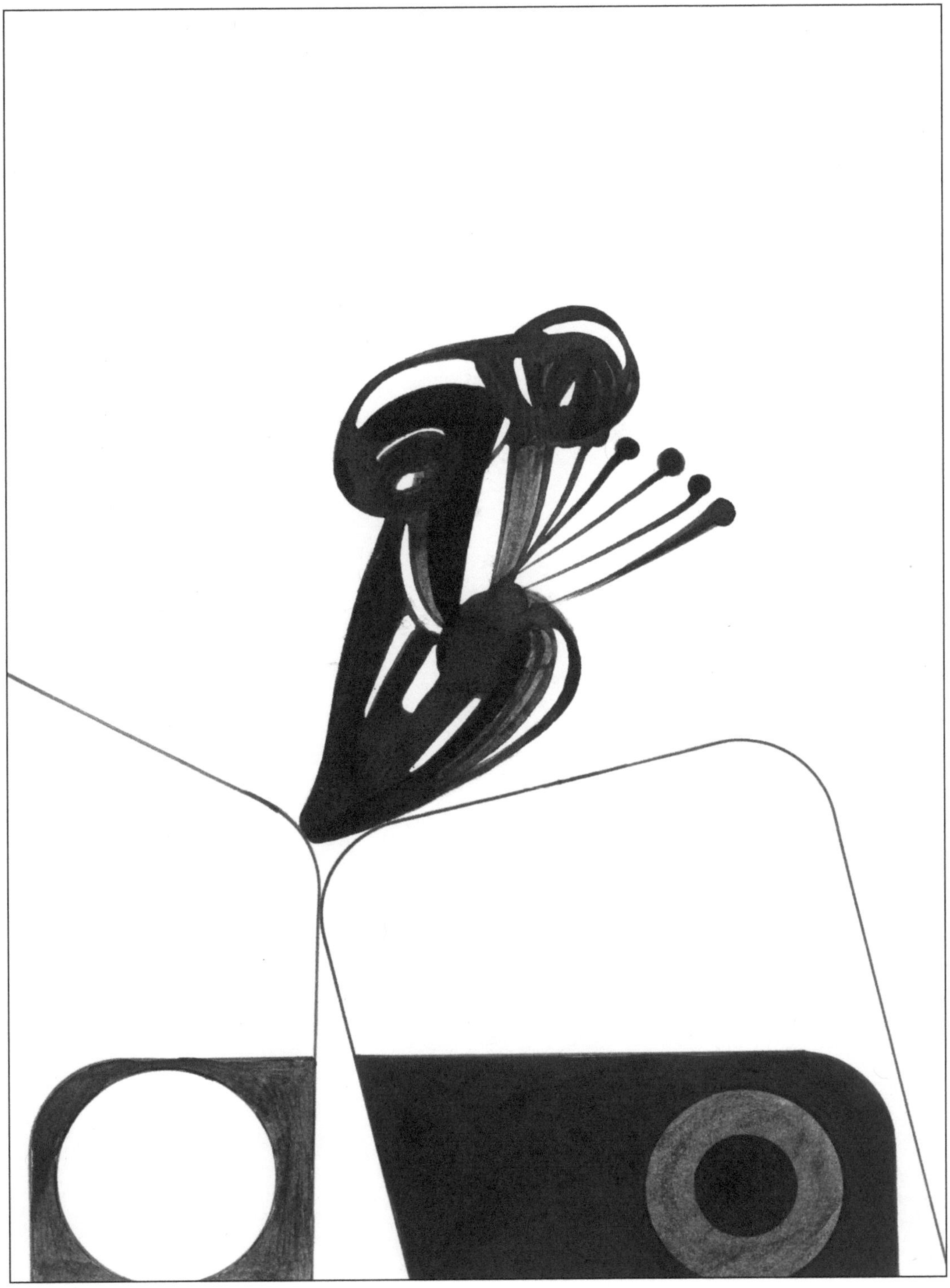

Eugene James Martin, untitled, s.d. (1981), 9 x 7"

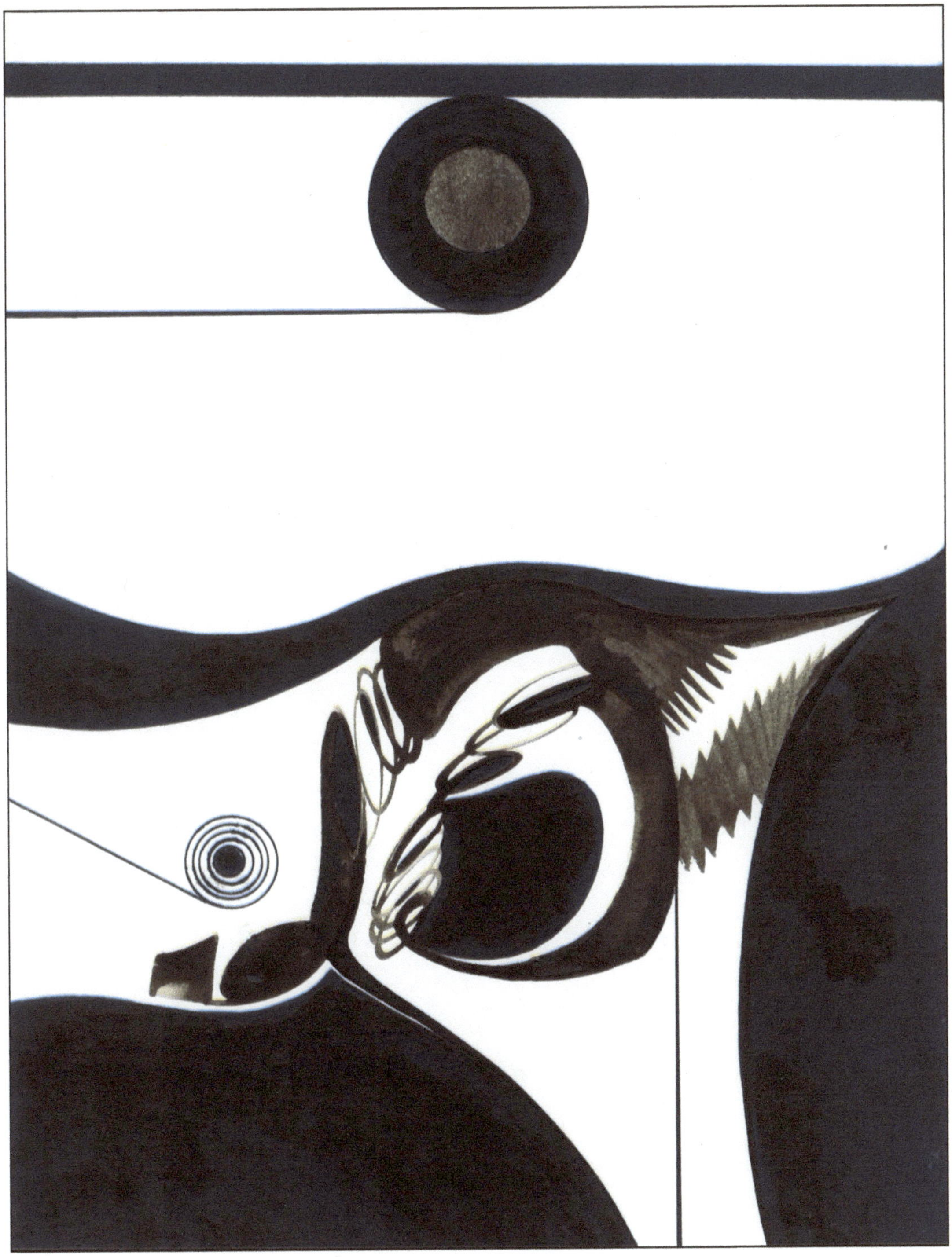

Eugene James Martin, untitled, 1982, 7 x 5.2"

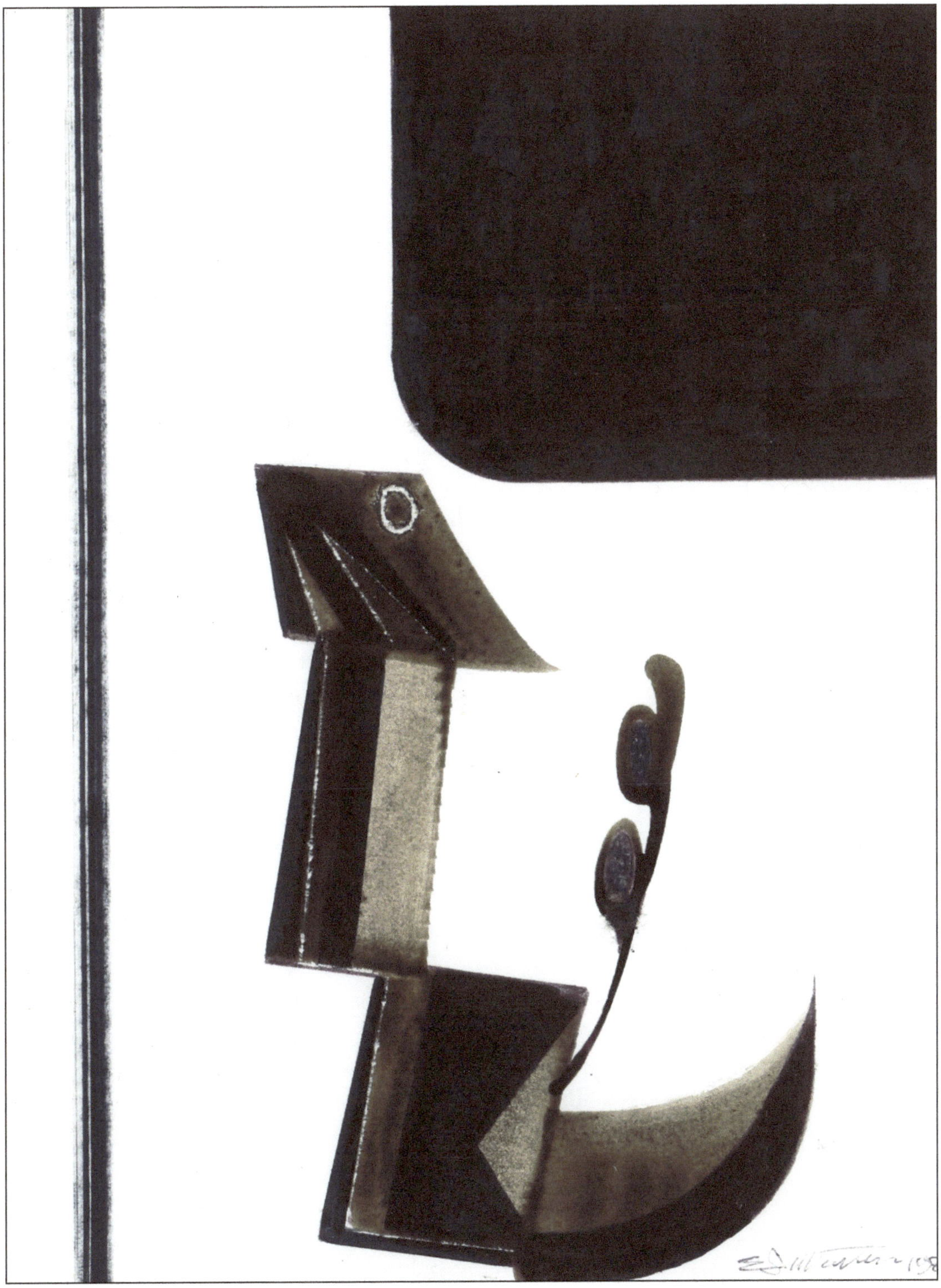

Eugene James Martin, untitled, 1982, 9.5 x 7"

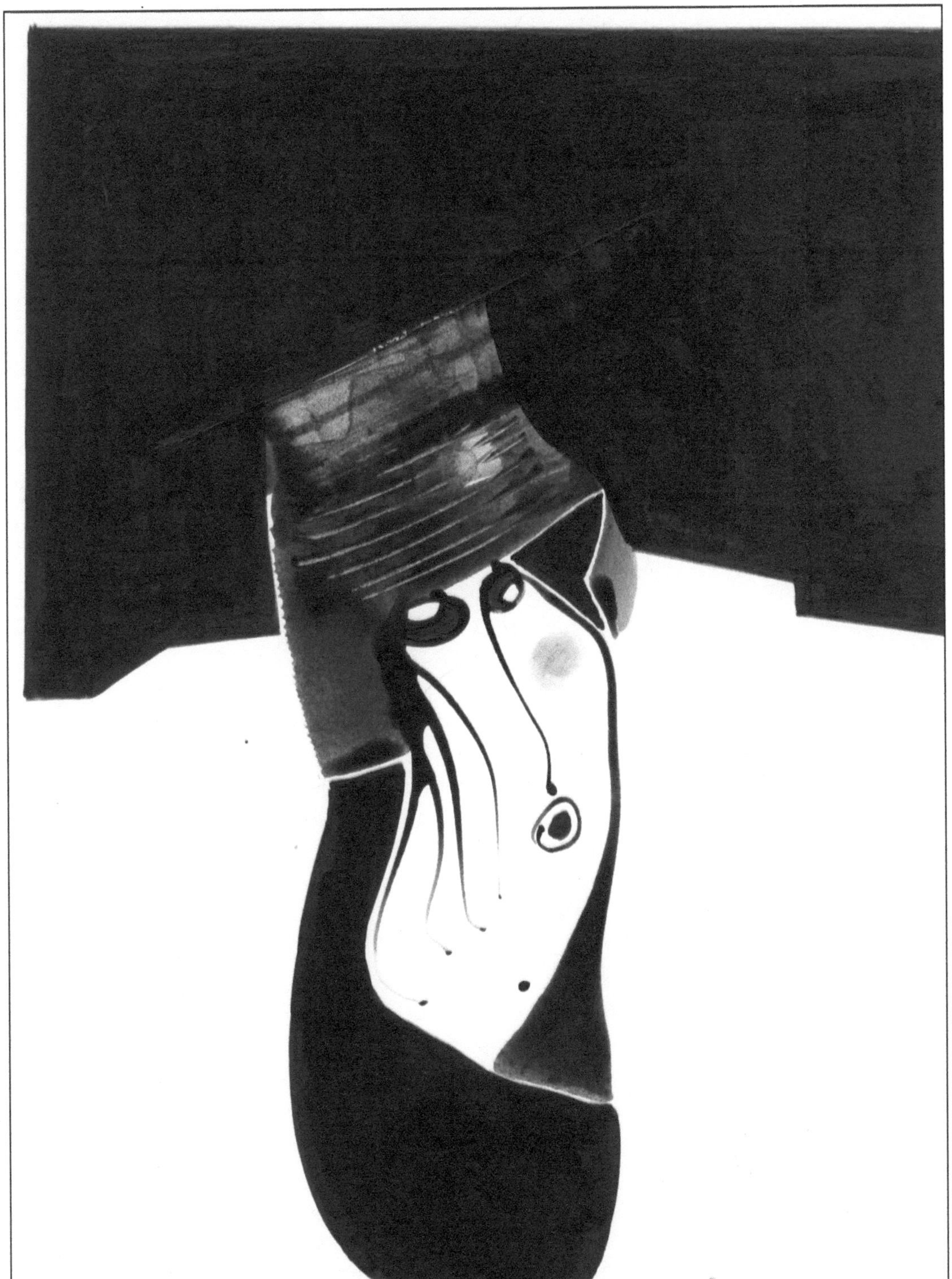

Eugene James Martin, untitled, 1981, 9.5 x 7"

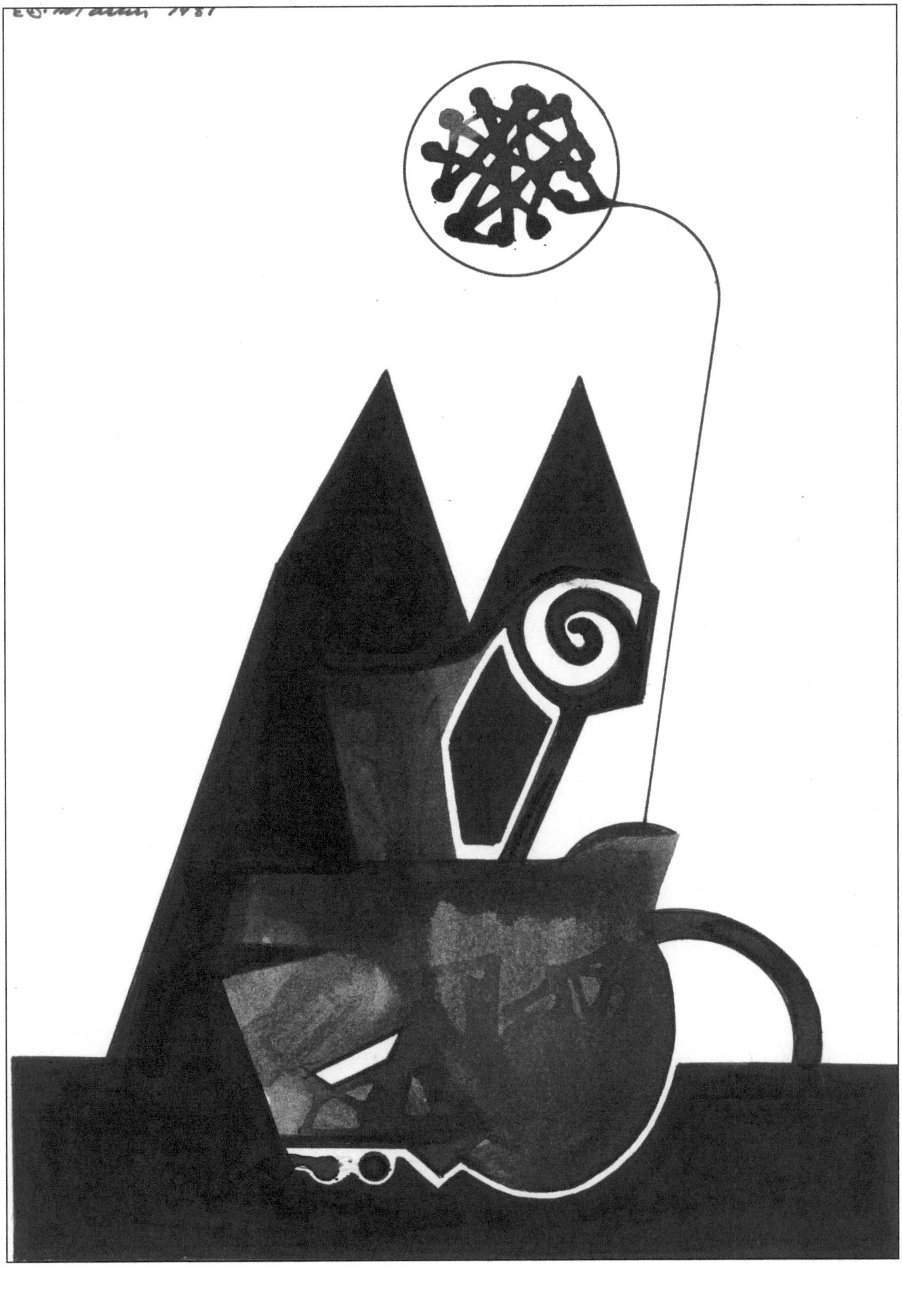

Eugene James Martin, untitled, s.d. (1981), 9.5 x 6.5"

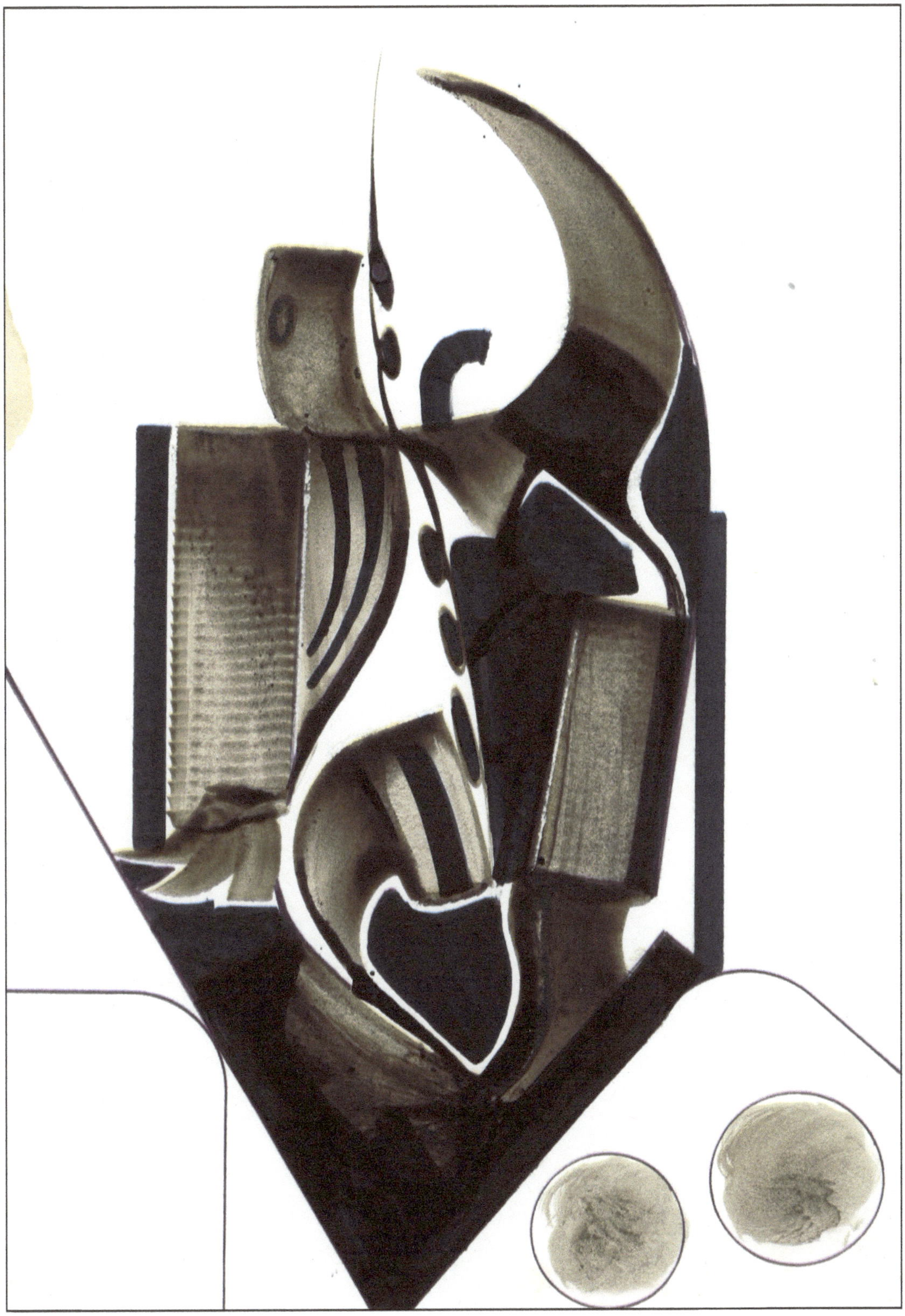

Eugene James Martin, untitled, s.d. (1981), 8.5 x 7"

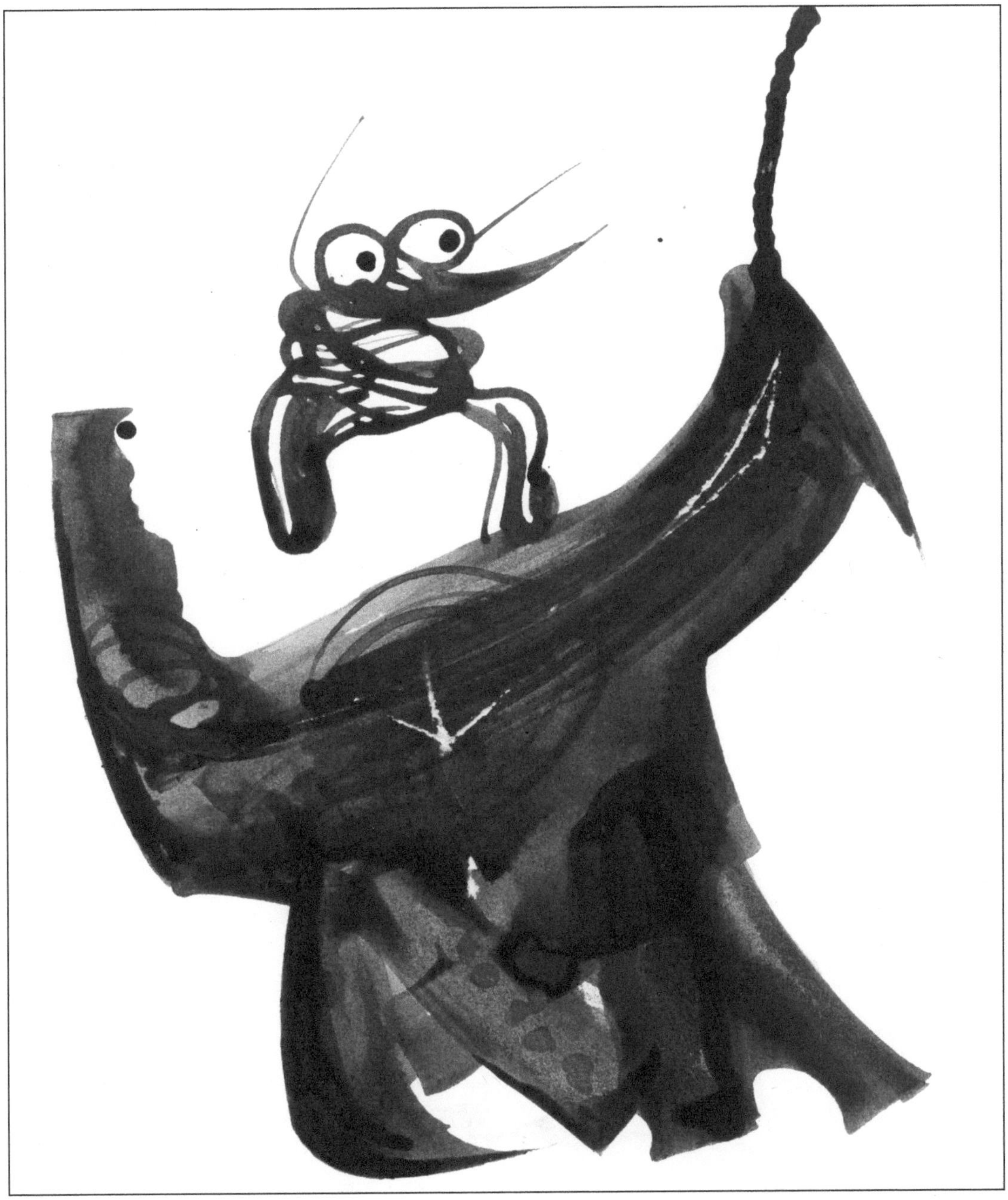

Eugene James Martin, untitled, 1981, 8 x 6.5"

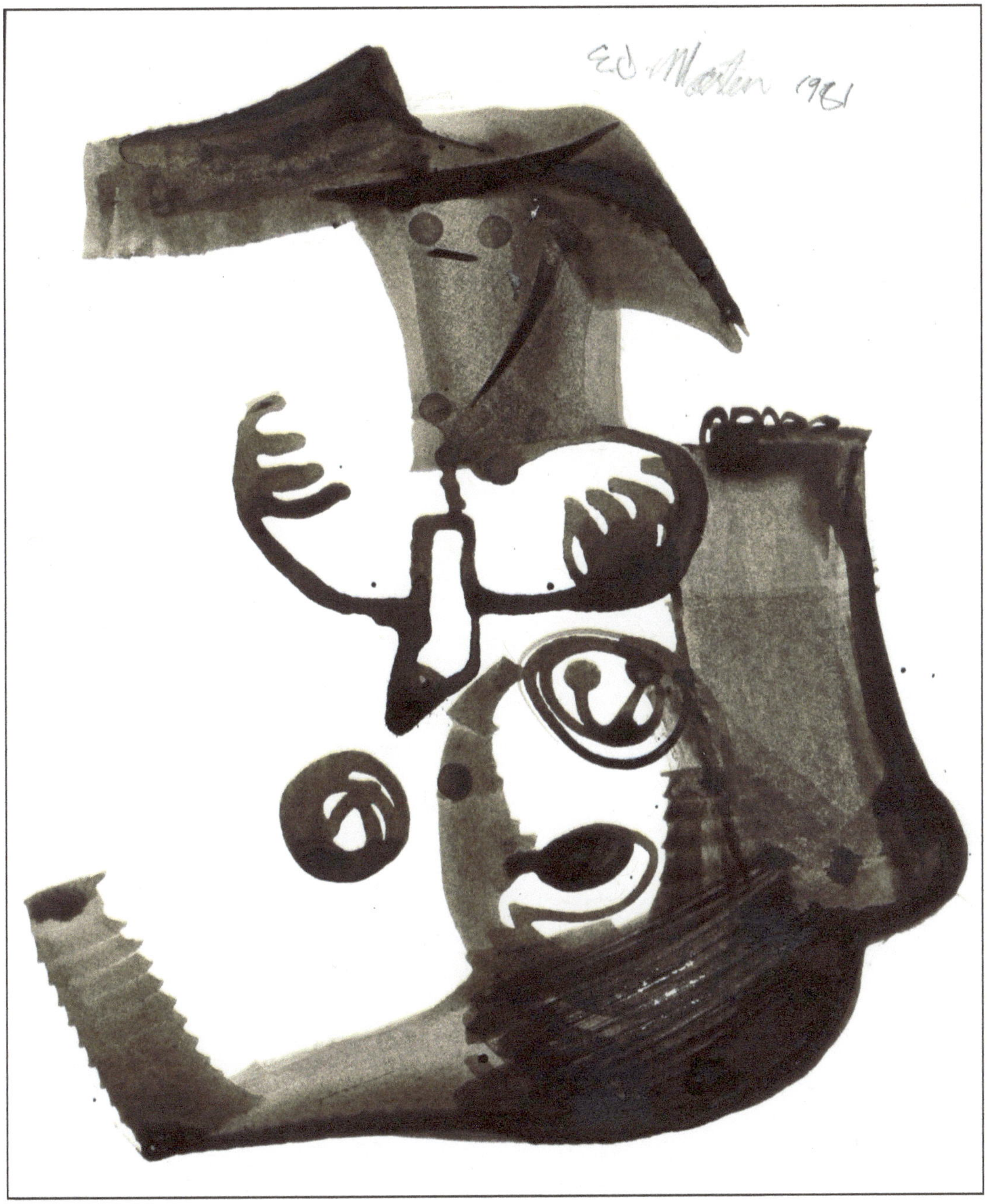
E.J. Martin 1961

Eugene James Martin, untitled, s.d. (1981), 8 x 5.8"

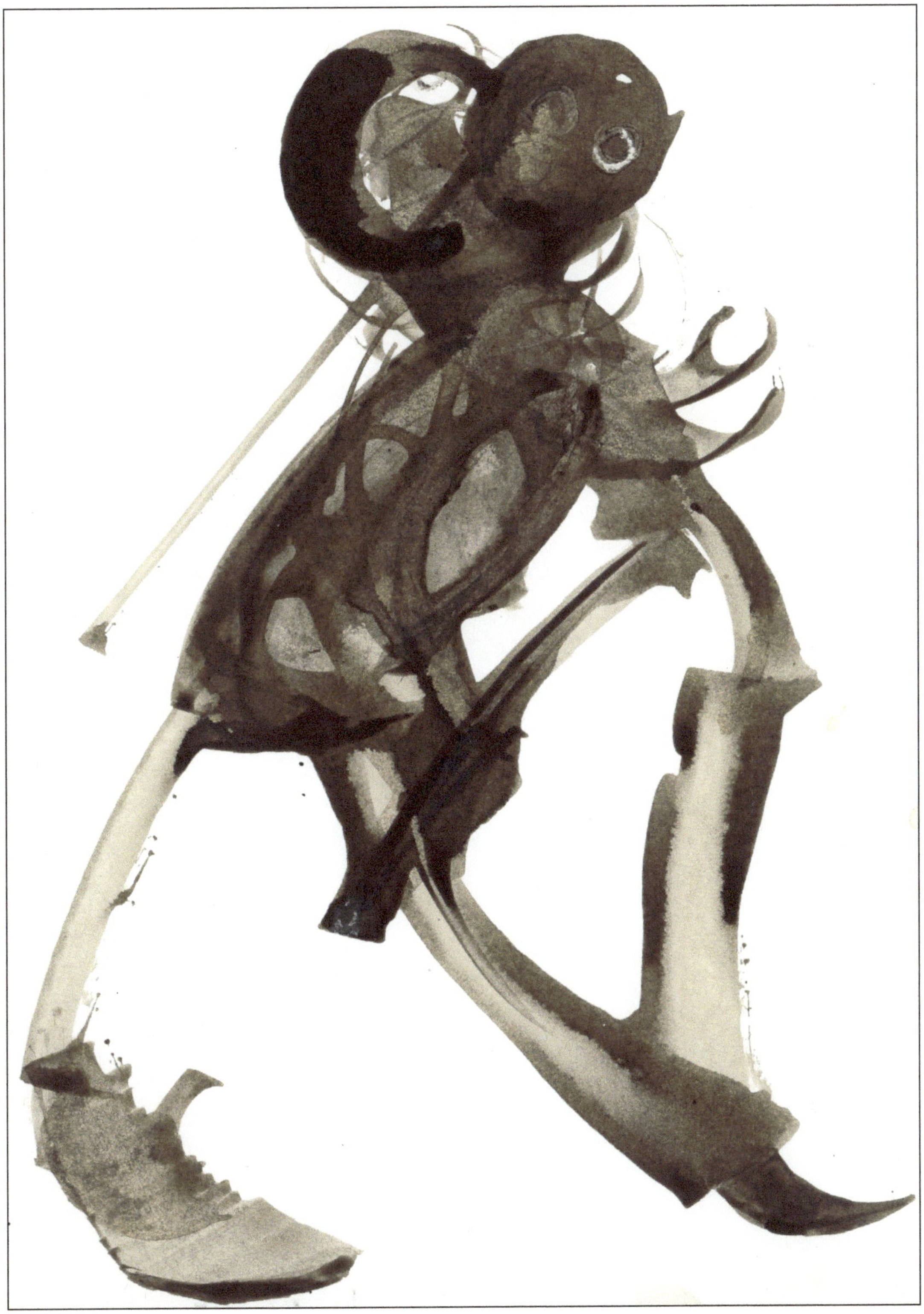

Eugene James Martin, untitled, 1981, 7.5 x 6.5"

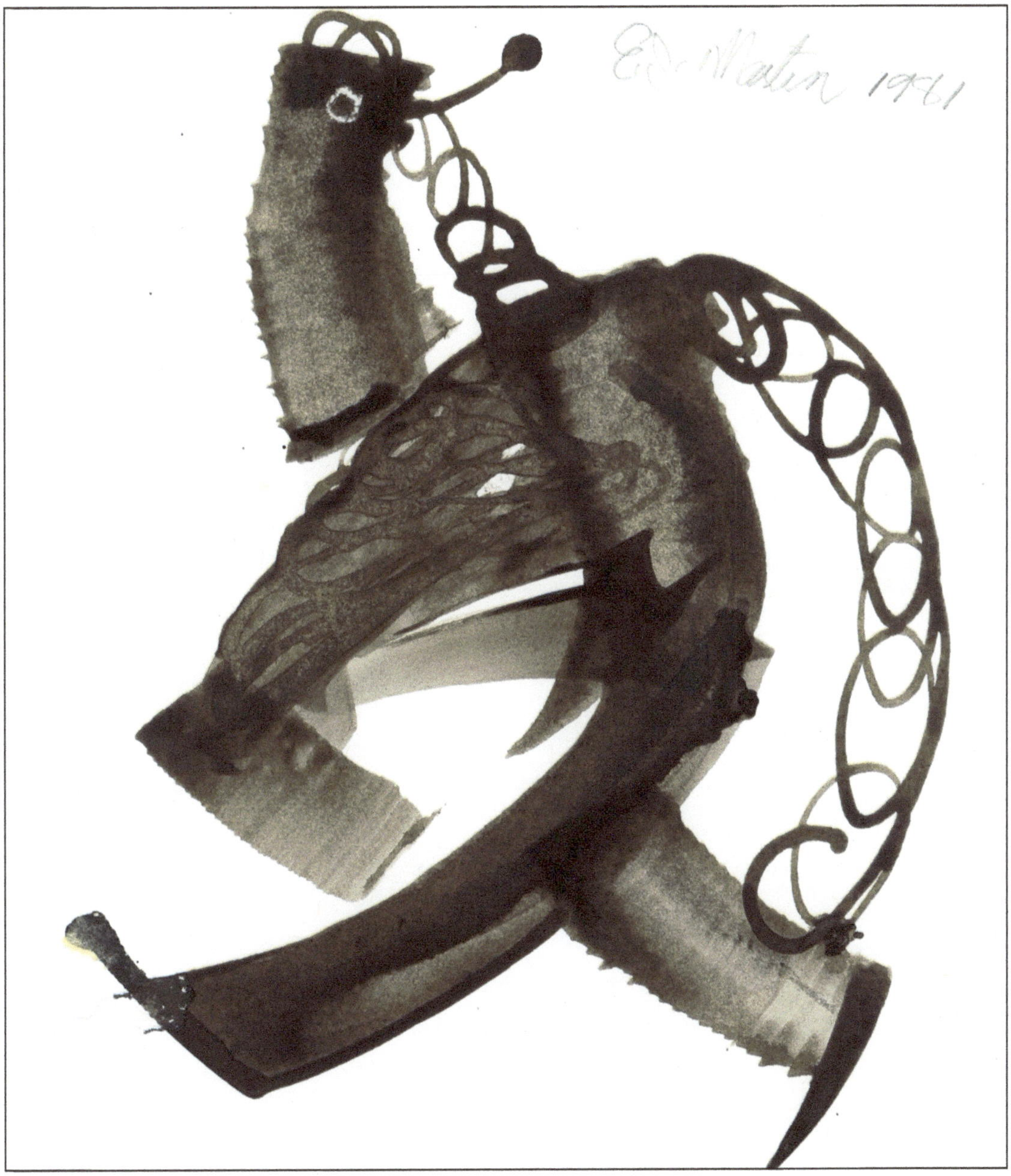

Eugene James Martin, untitled, 1982, 9.5 x 7"

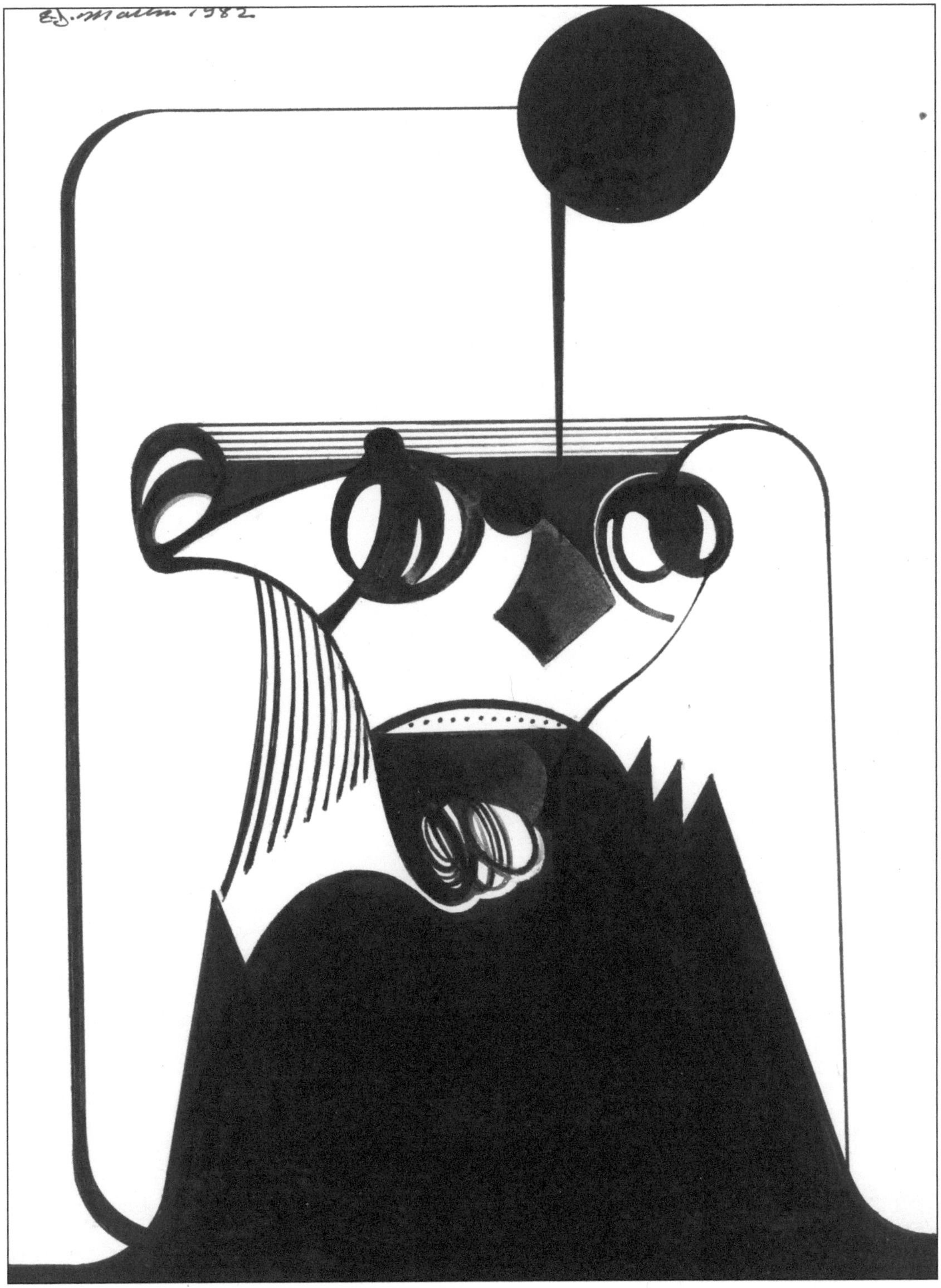

Eugene James Martin, untitled, 1982, 9.8 x 7"

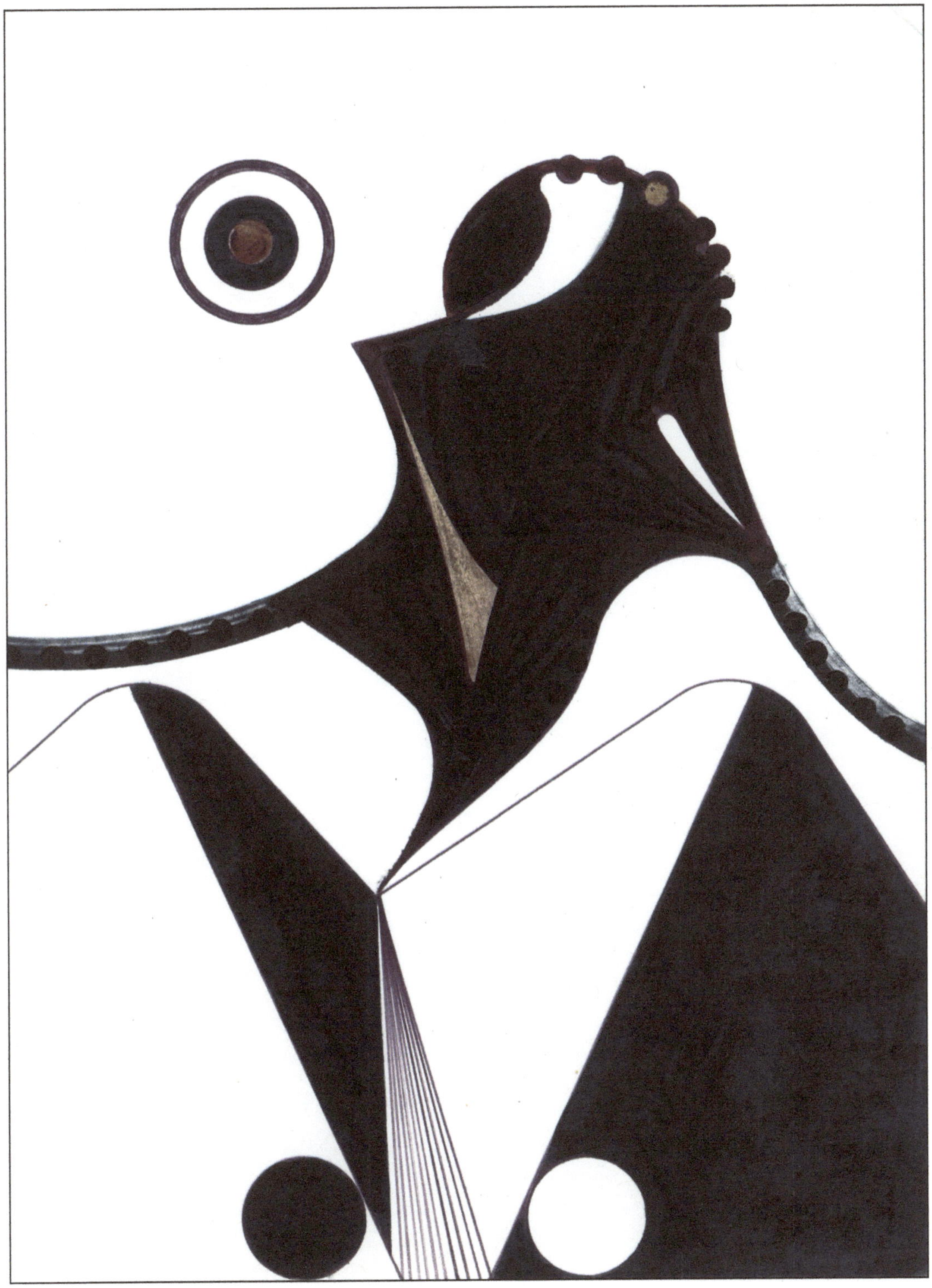

Eugene James Martin, untitled, s.d. (1981), 9.5 x 7"

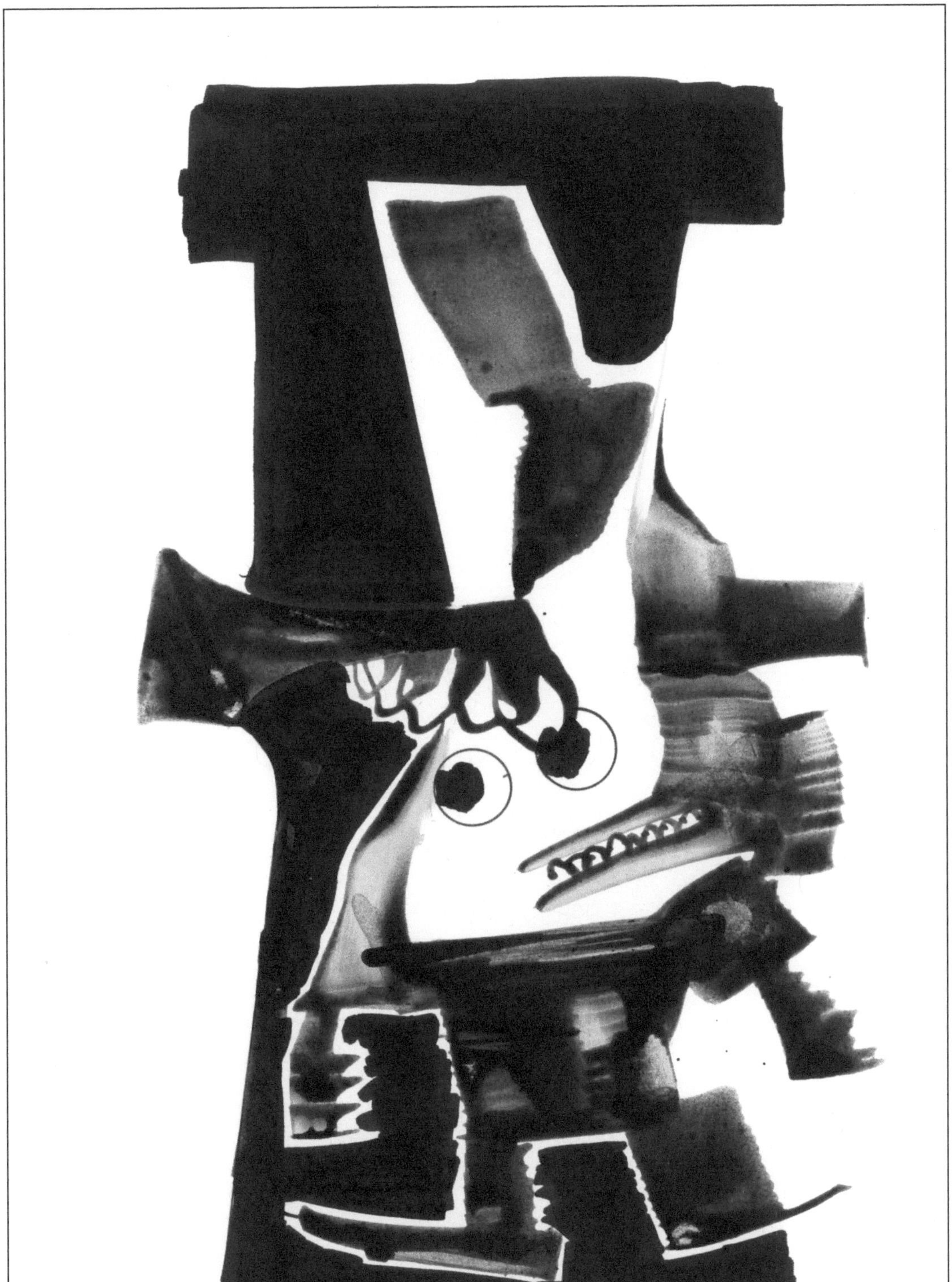

Eugene James Martin, untitled, 1982, 7.8 x 5"

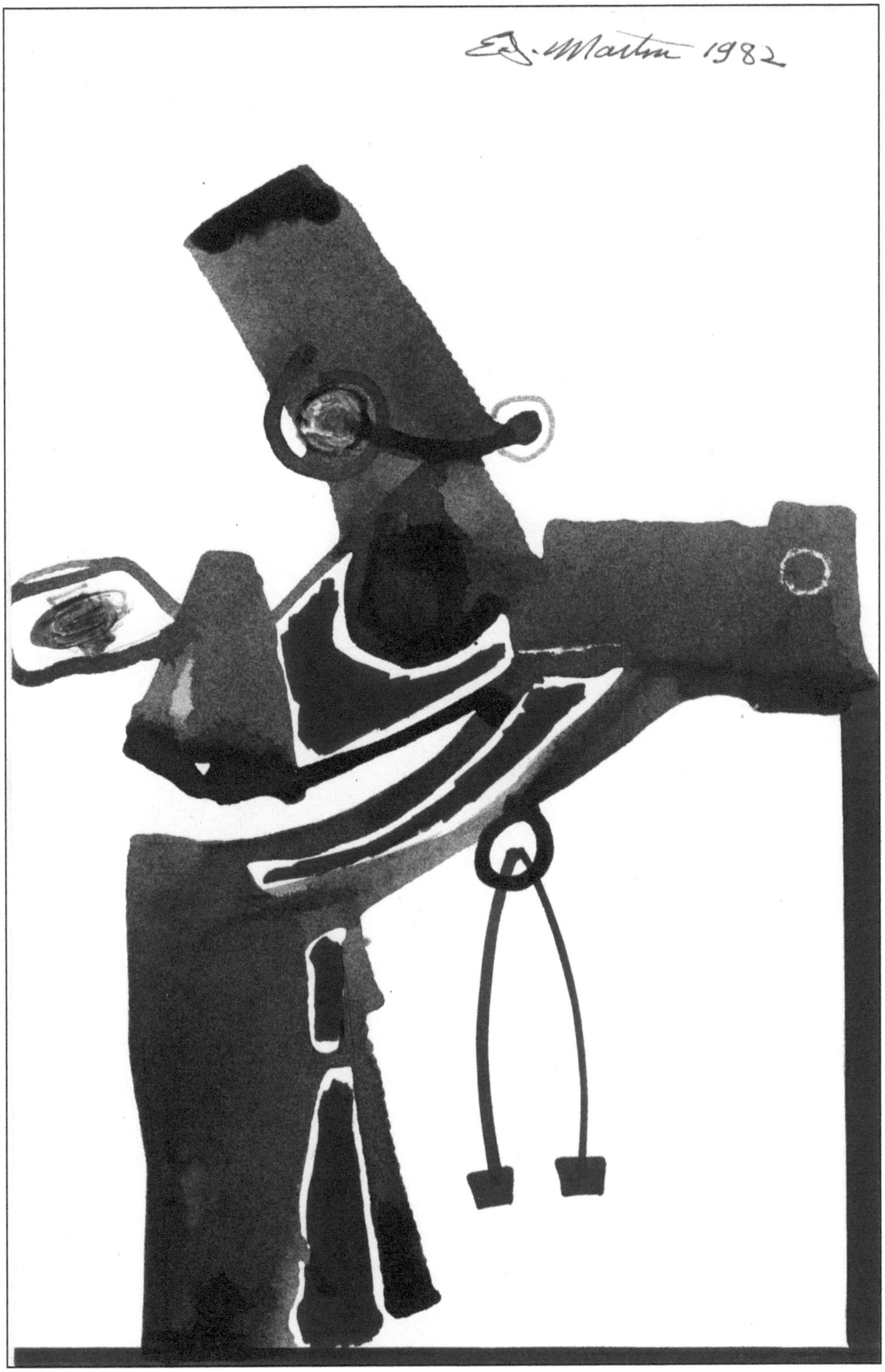
E.J. Martin 1982

Eugene James Martin, untitled, s.d. (1981), 9 x 7"

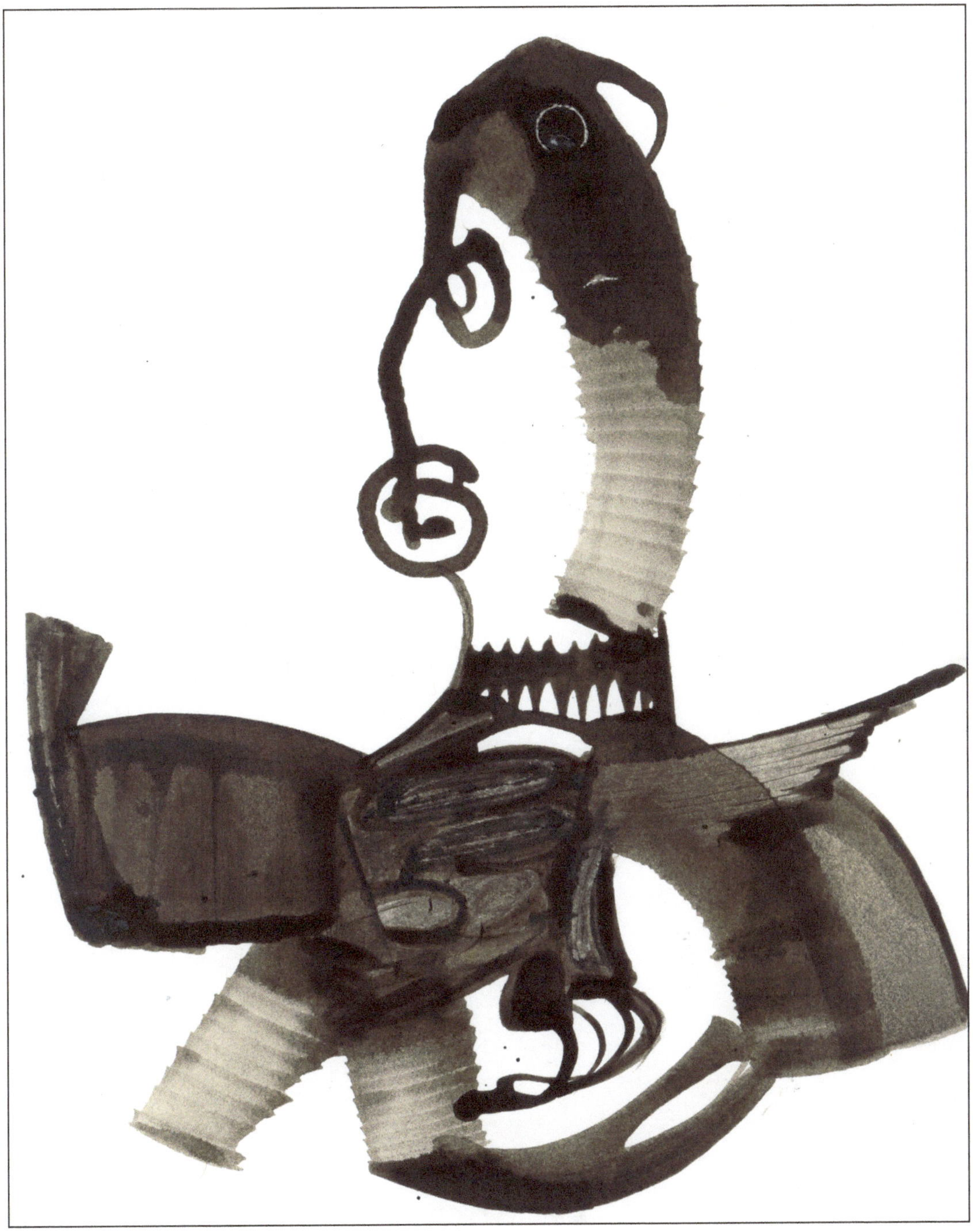

Eugene James Martin, untitled, 1981, 9 x 7"

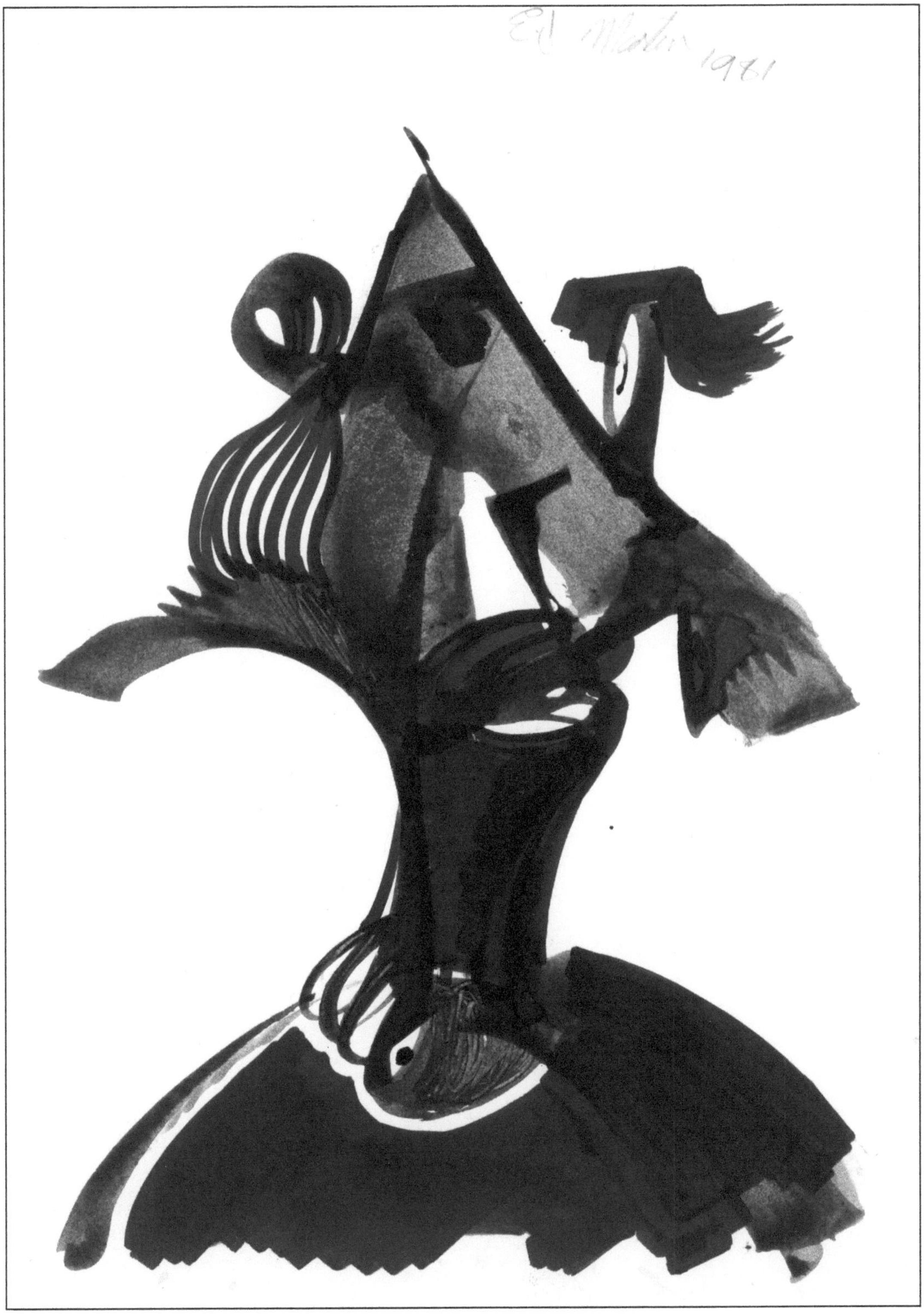

Eugene James Martin, untitled, s.d. (1981), 9.5 x 7"

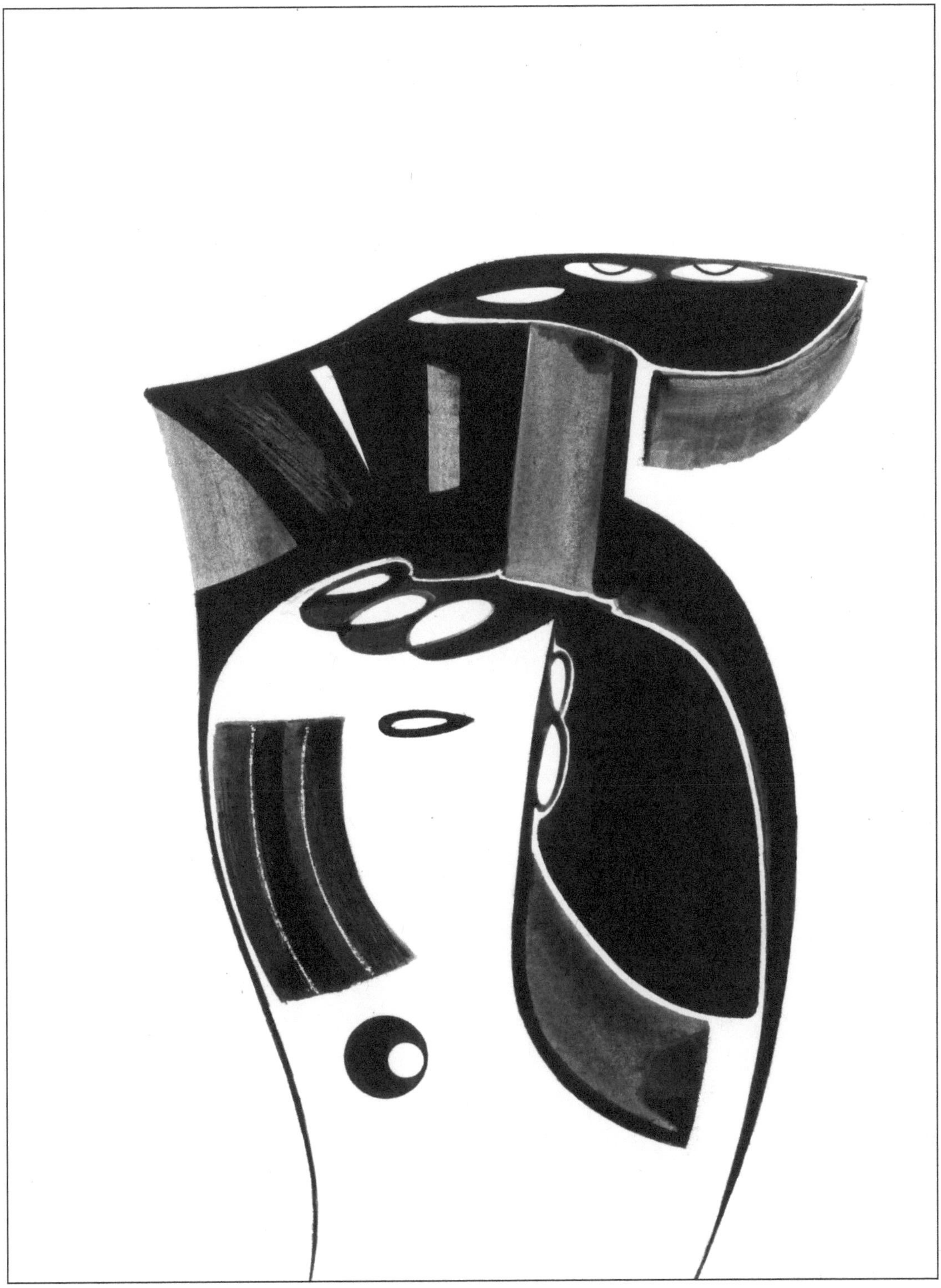

Eugene James Martin, untitled, 1982, 9 x 7.2"

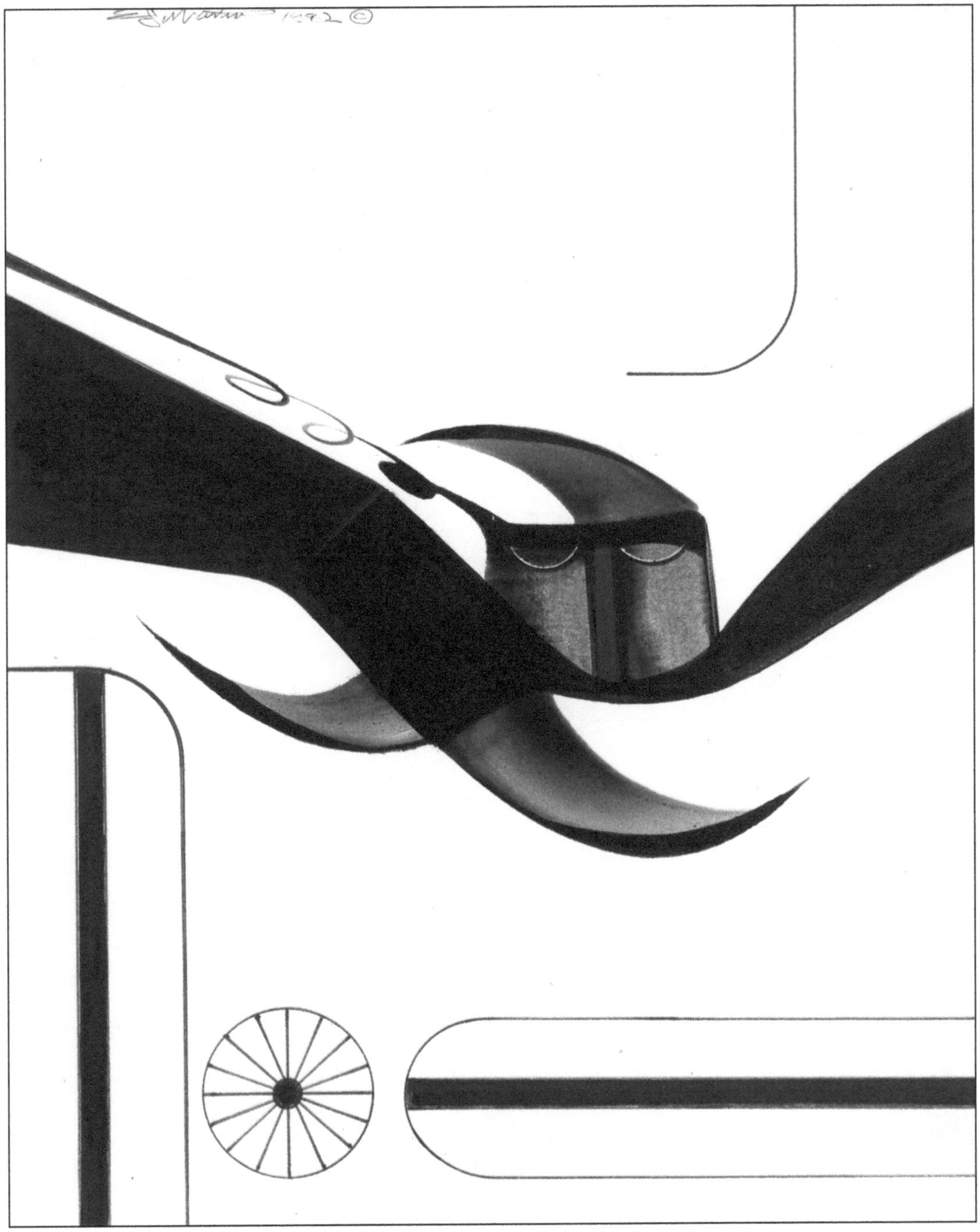

Eugene James Martin, untitled, 1981, 9.5 x 6.8"

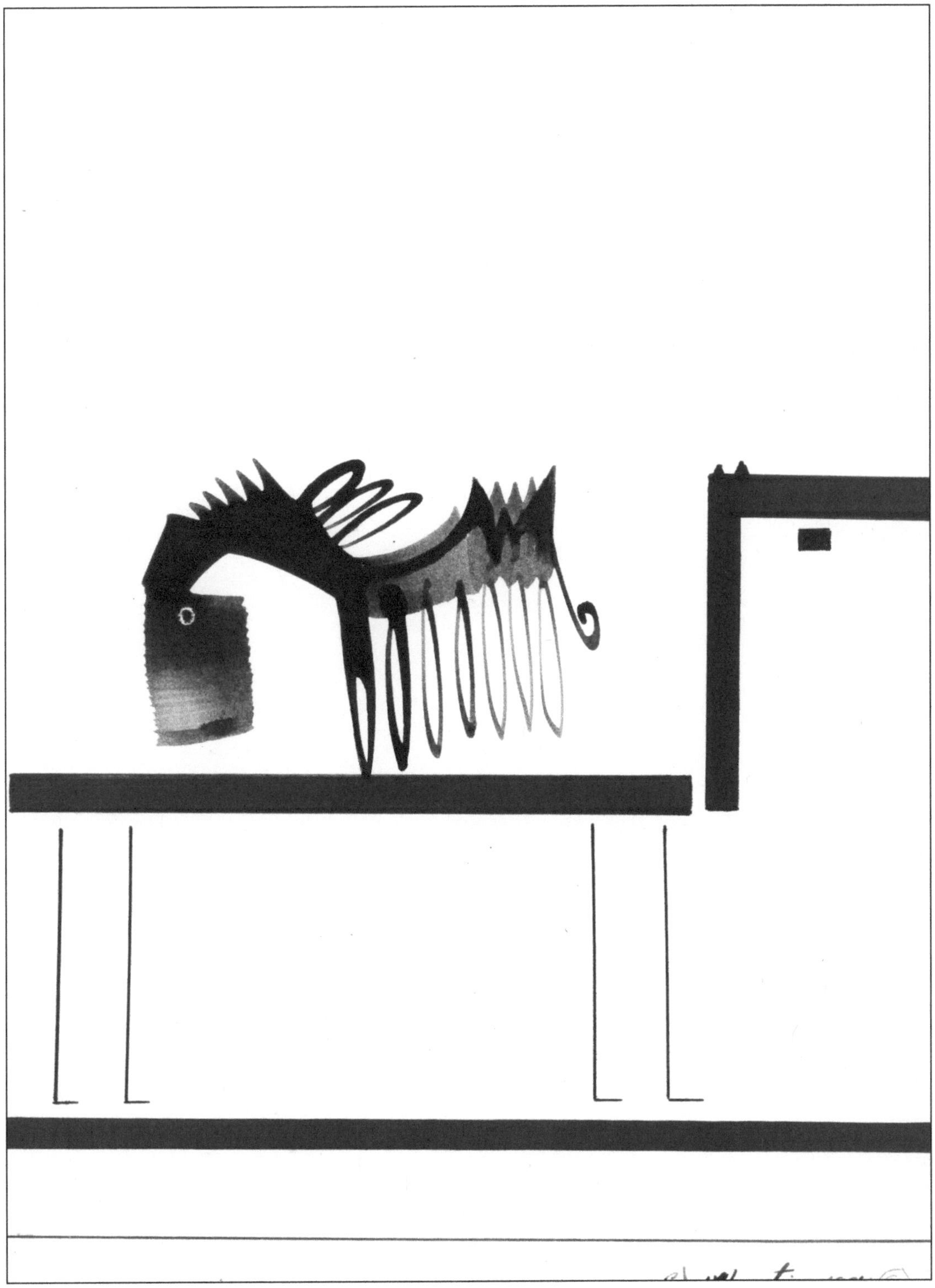

Eugene James Martin, untitled, 1981, 5 x 6.8"

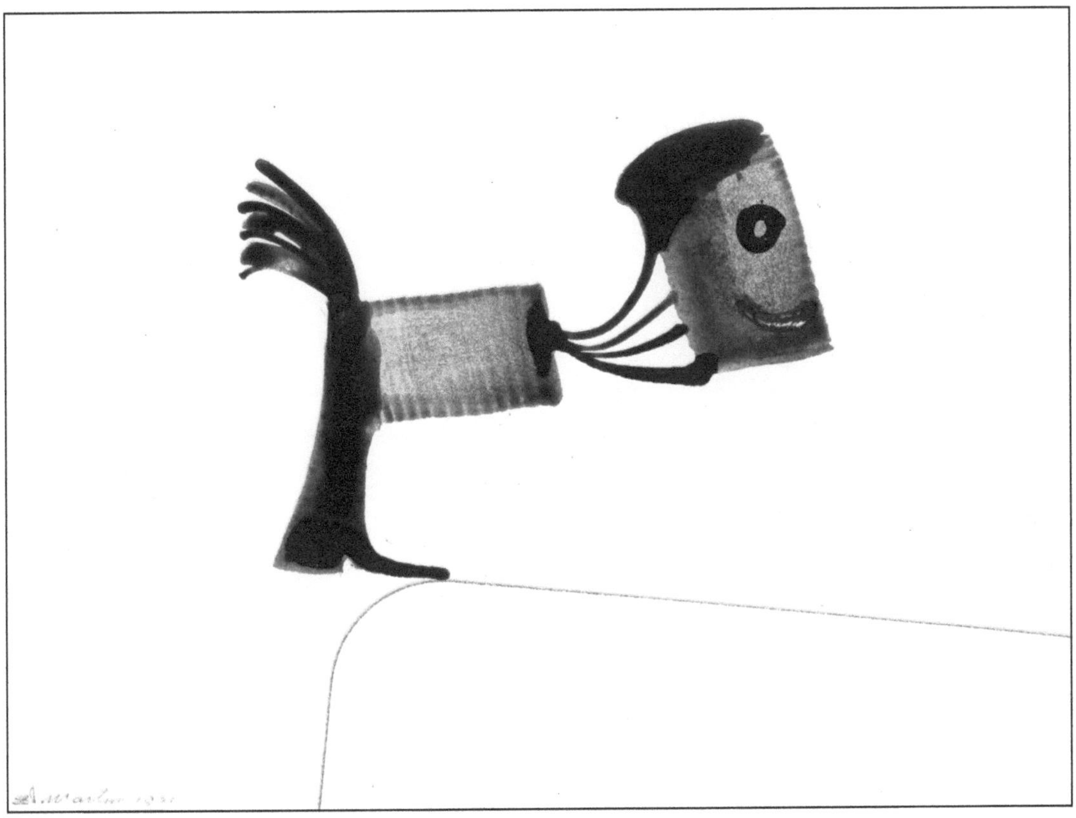

Eugene James Martin, untitled, 1982, 7.5 x 5.5"

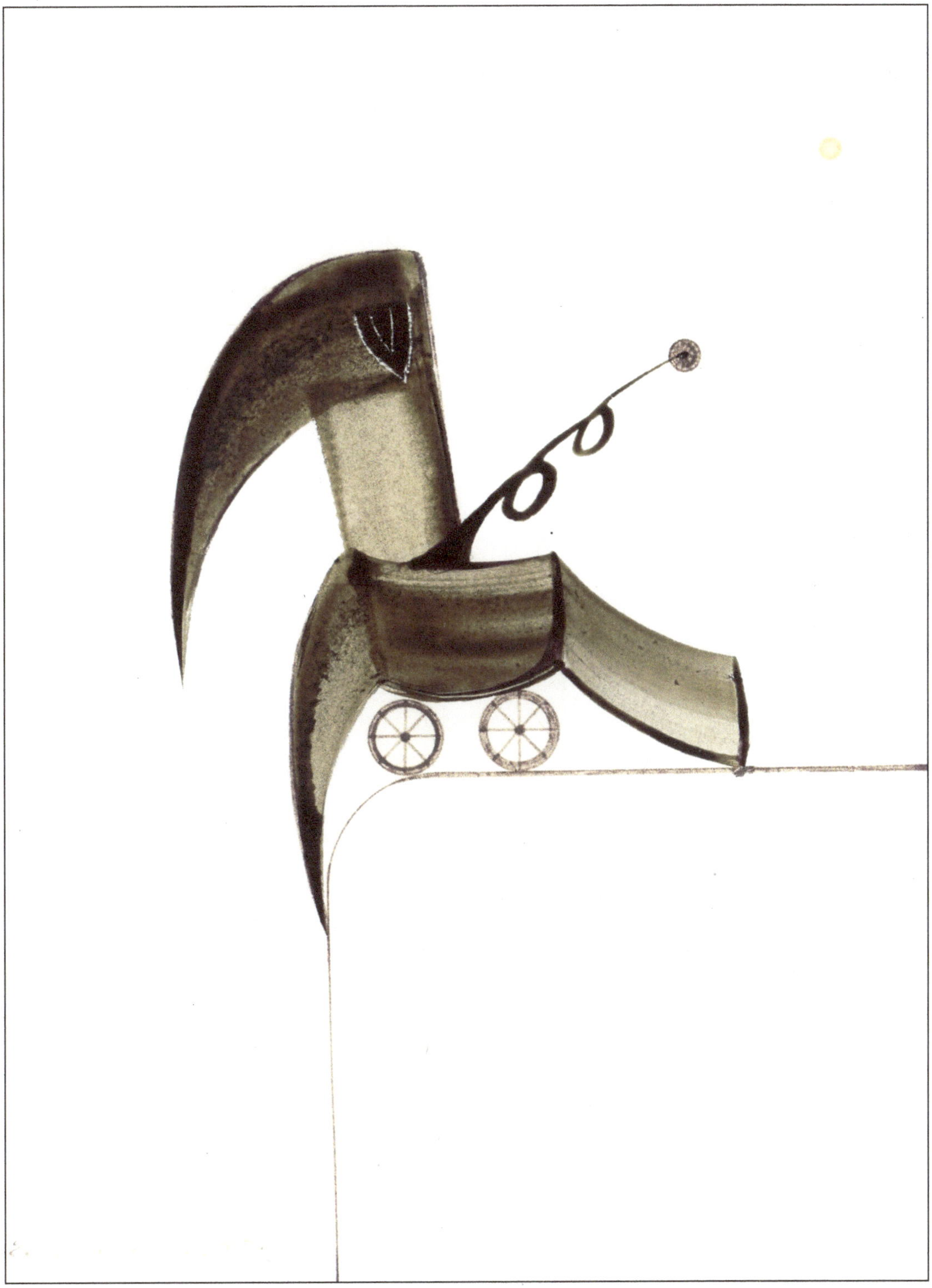

Eugene James Martin, untitled, 1982, 9 x 6.5"

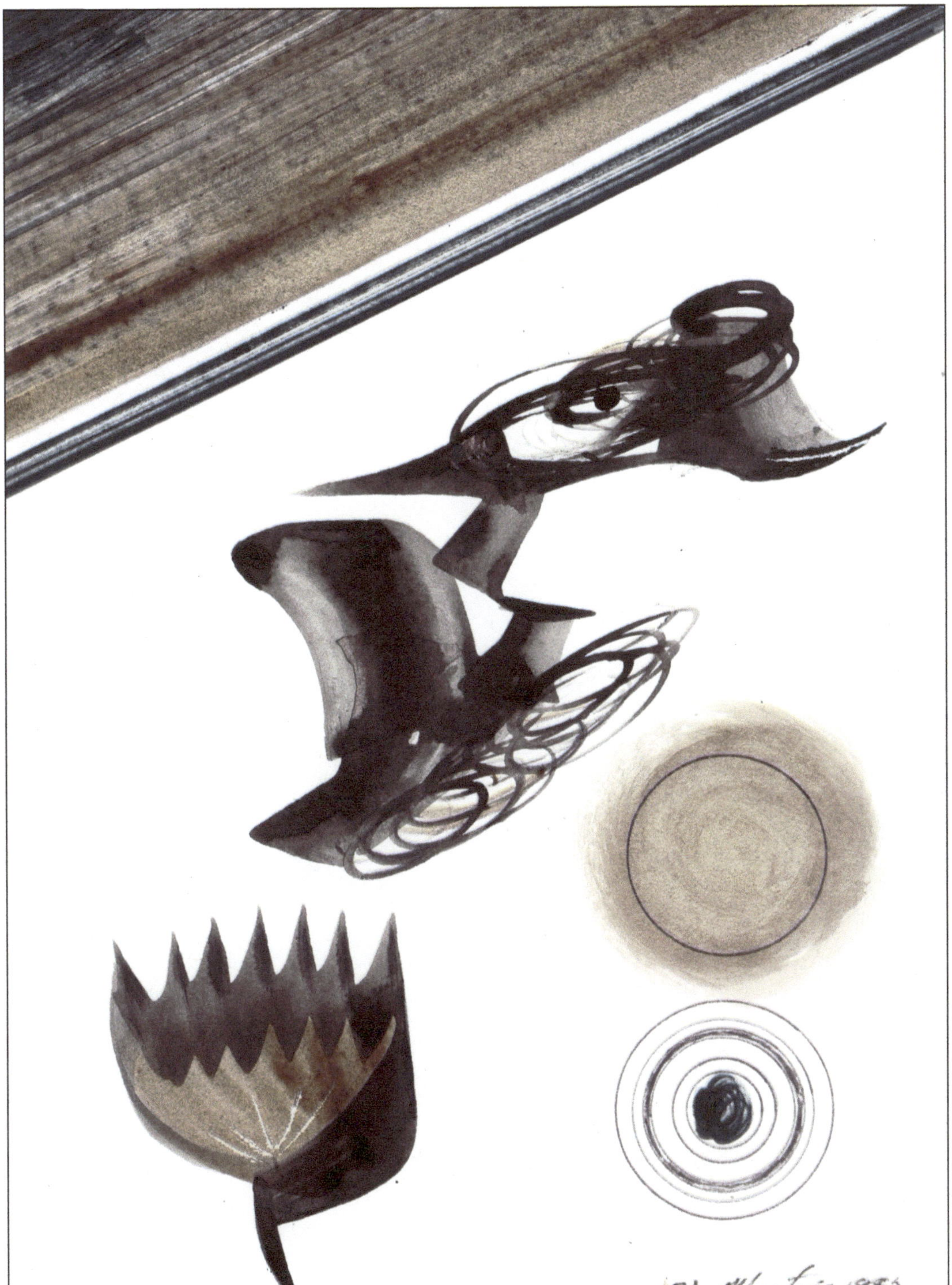

Eugene James Martin, Ice Hockey, 1982, 8.5 x 7"

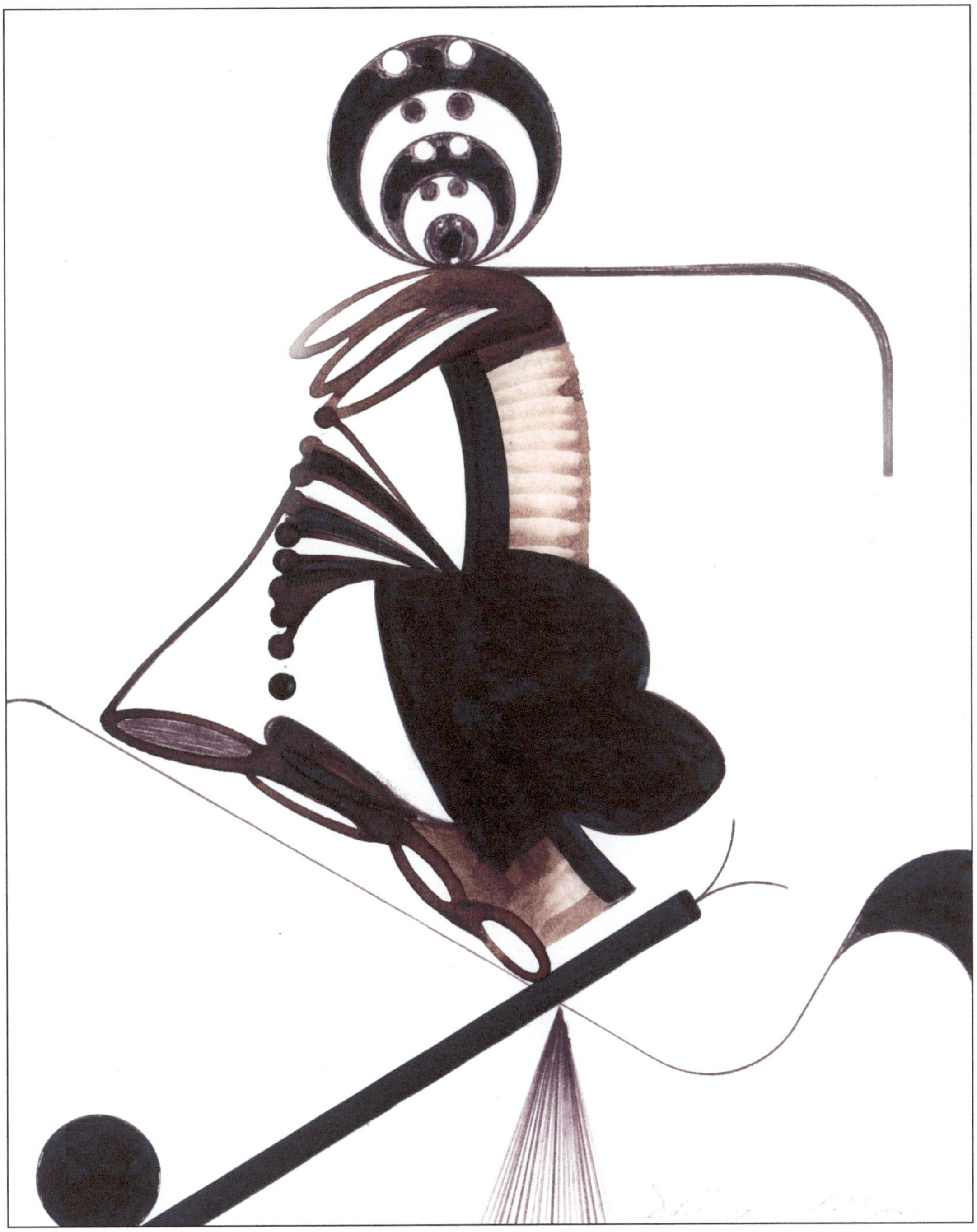

Eugene James Martin, untitled, 1981, 8.5 x 6.5"

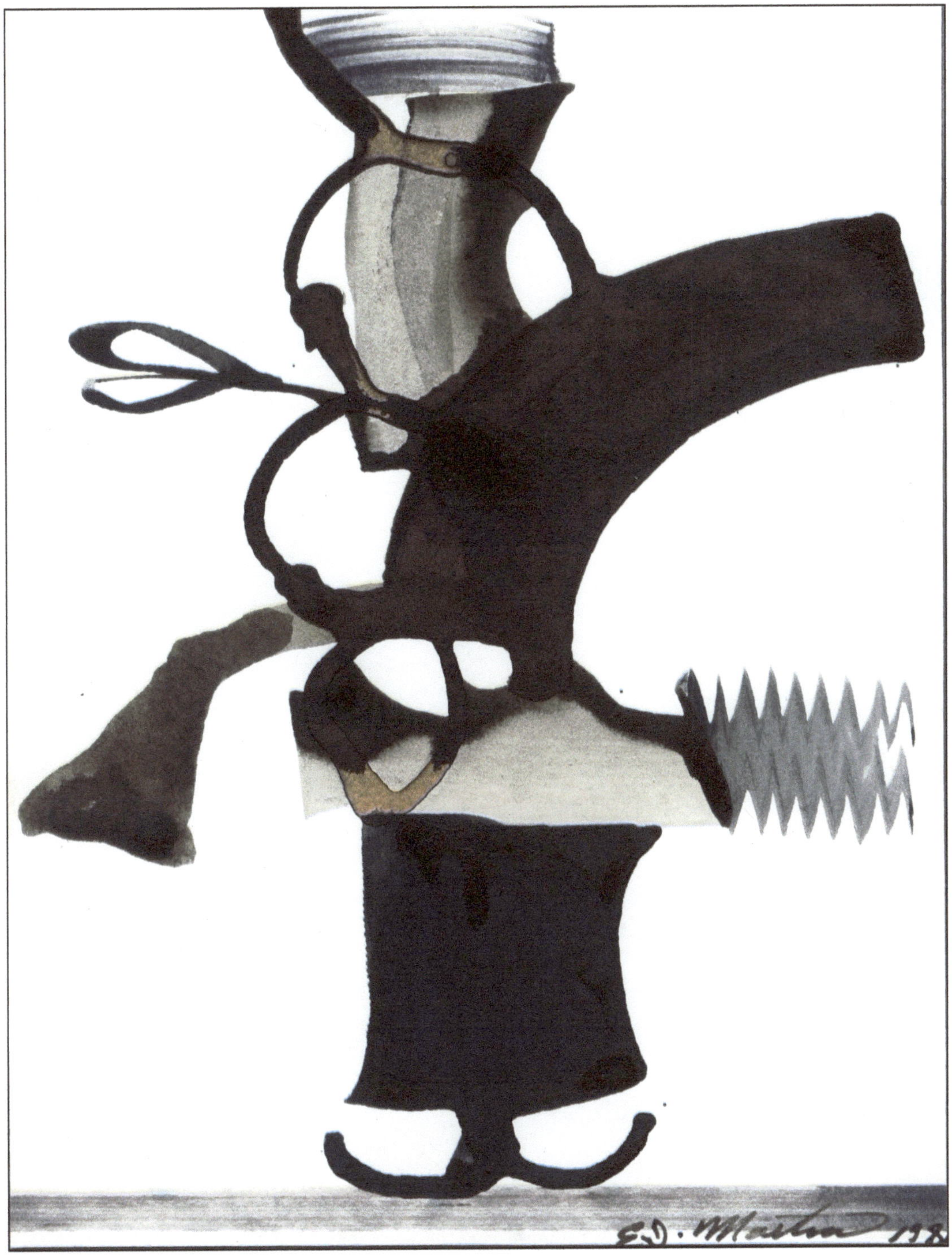
E.J. Martin 98

Eugene James Martin, untitled, 1982, 9.8 x 7"

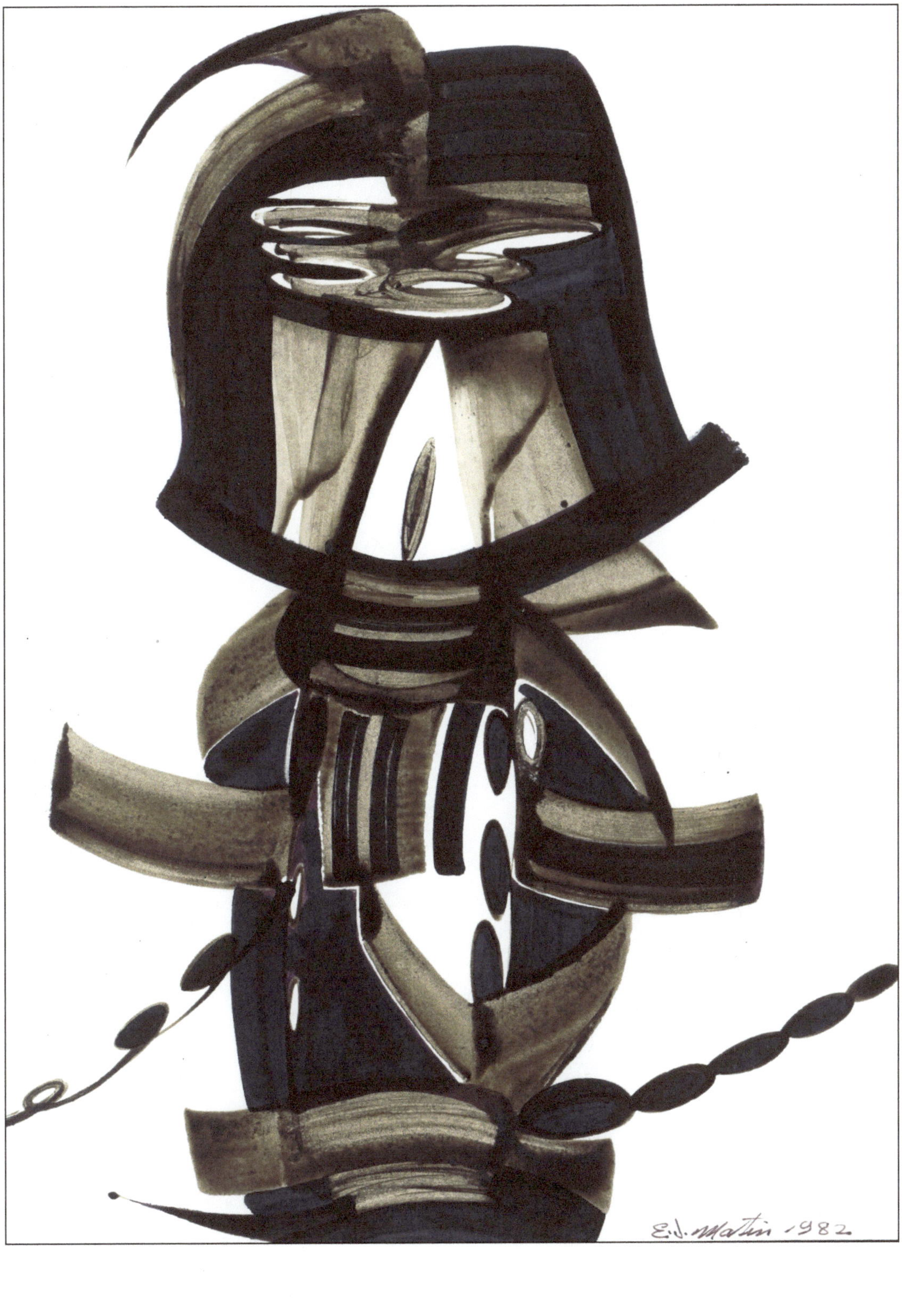
E.J. Martin 1982

Eugene James Martin, untitled, s.d. (1982), 8.5 x 6.5

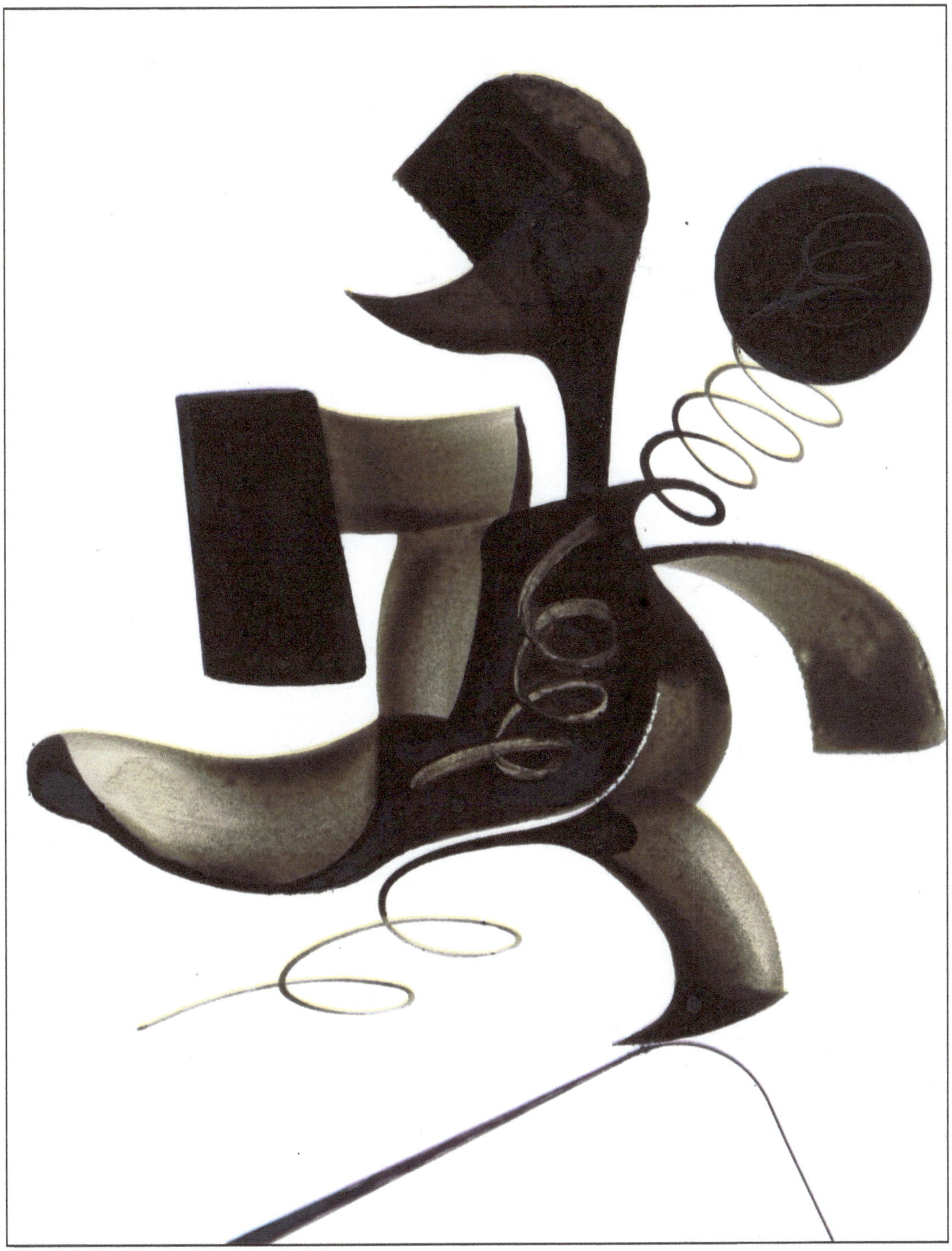

Eugene James Martin, untitled, s.d. (1981), 9.8 x 7"

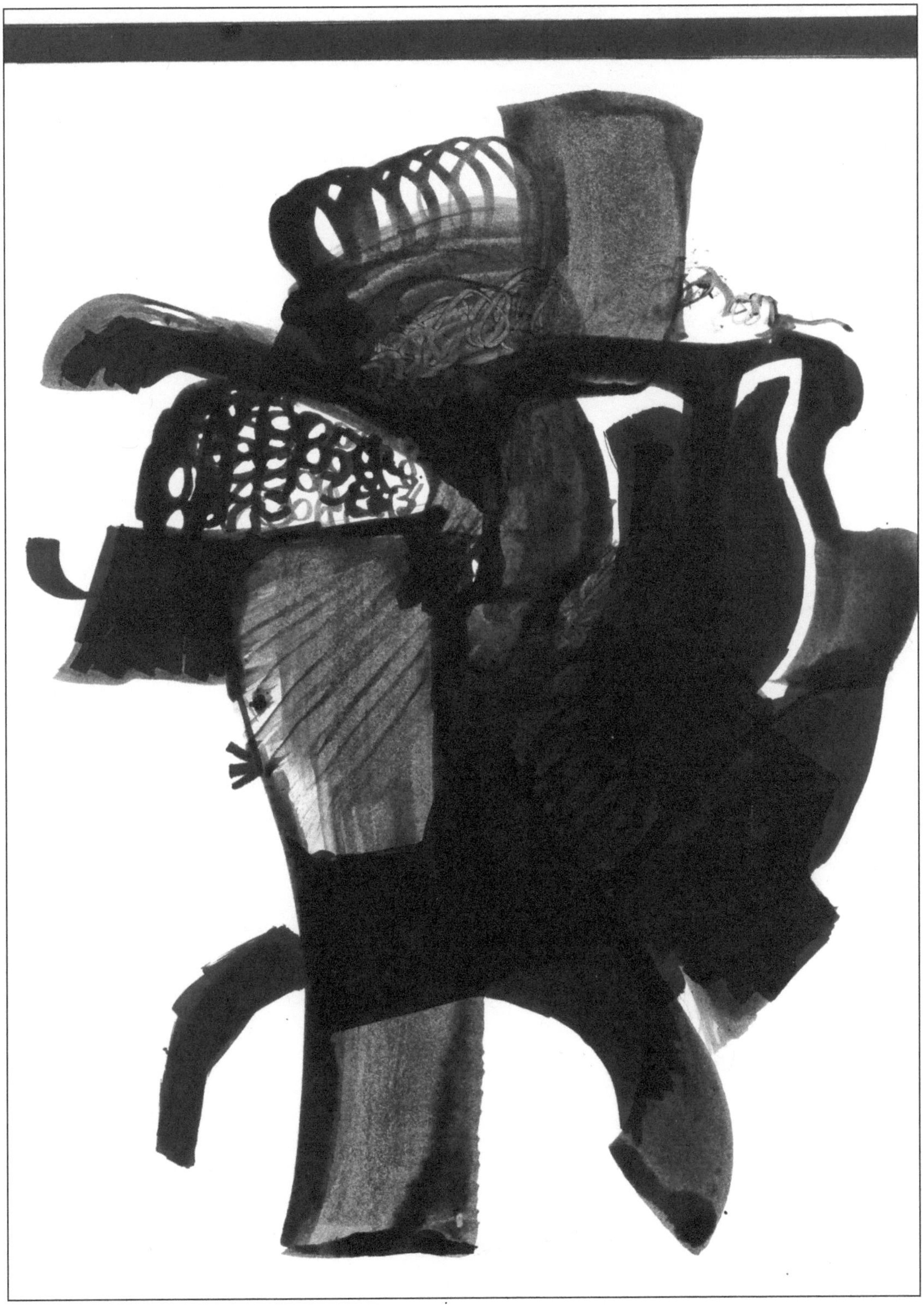

Eugene James Martin, Substance to Success, 1981, 9.5 x 7"

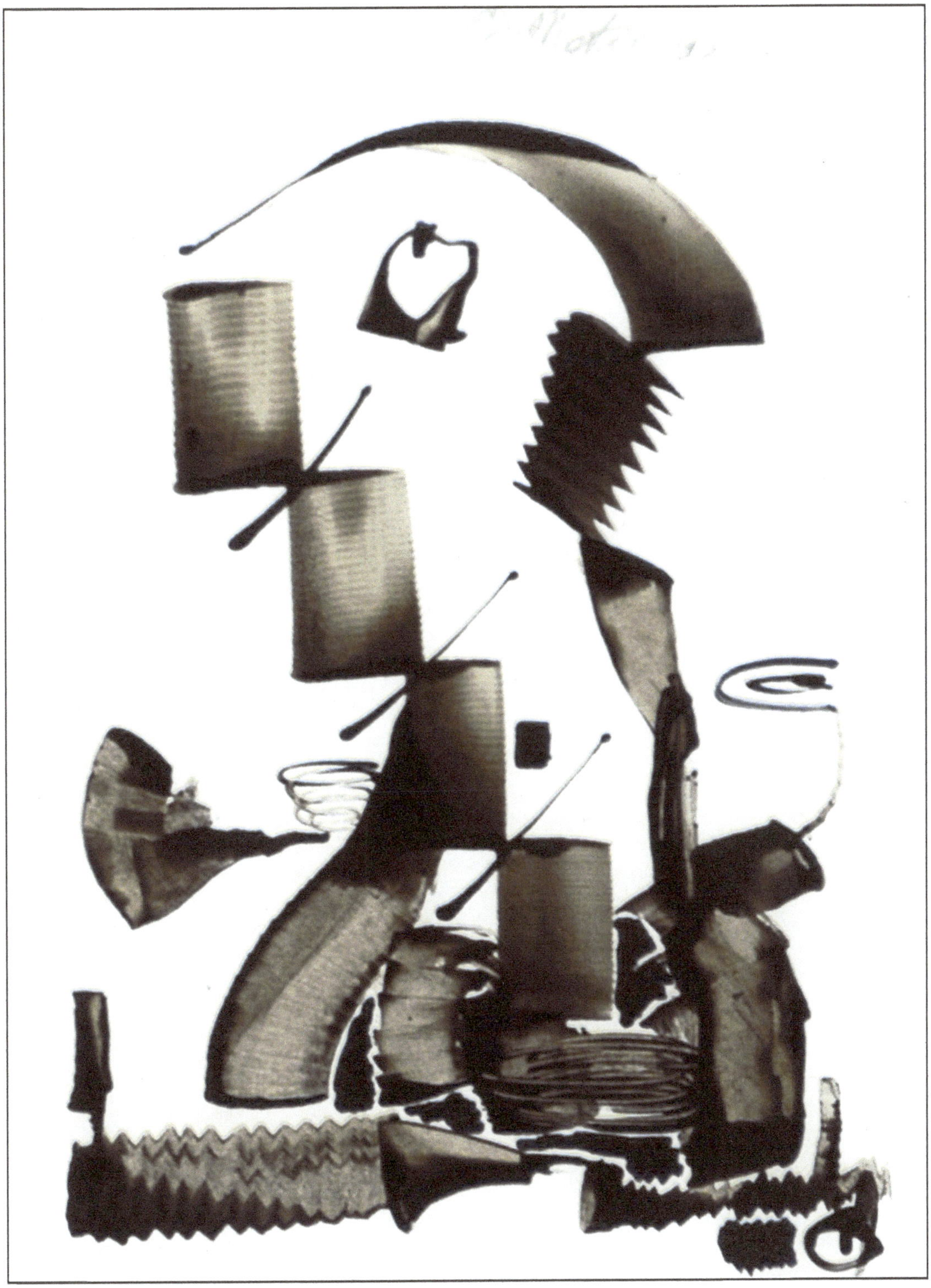

Eugene James Martin, untitled, s.d. (1981), 8 x 6.5"

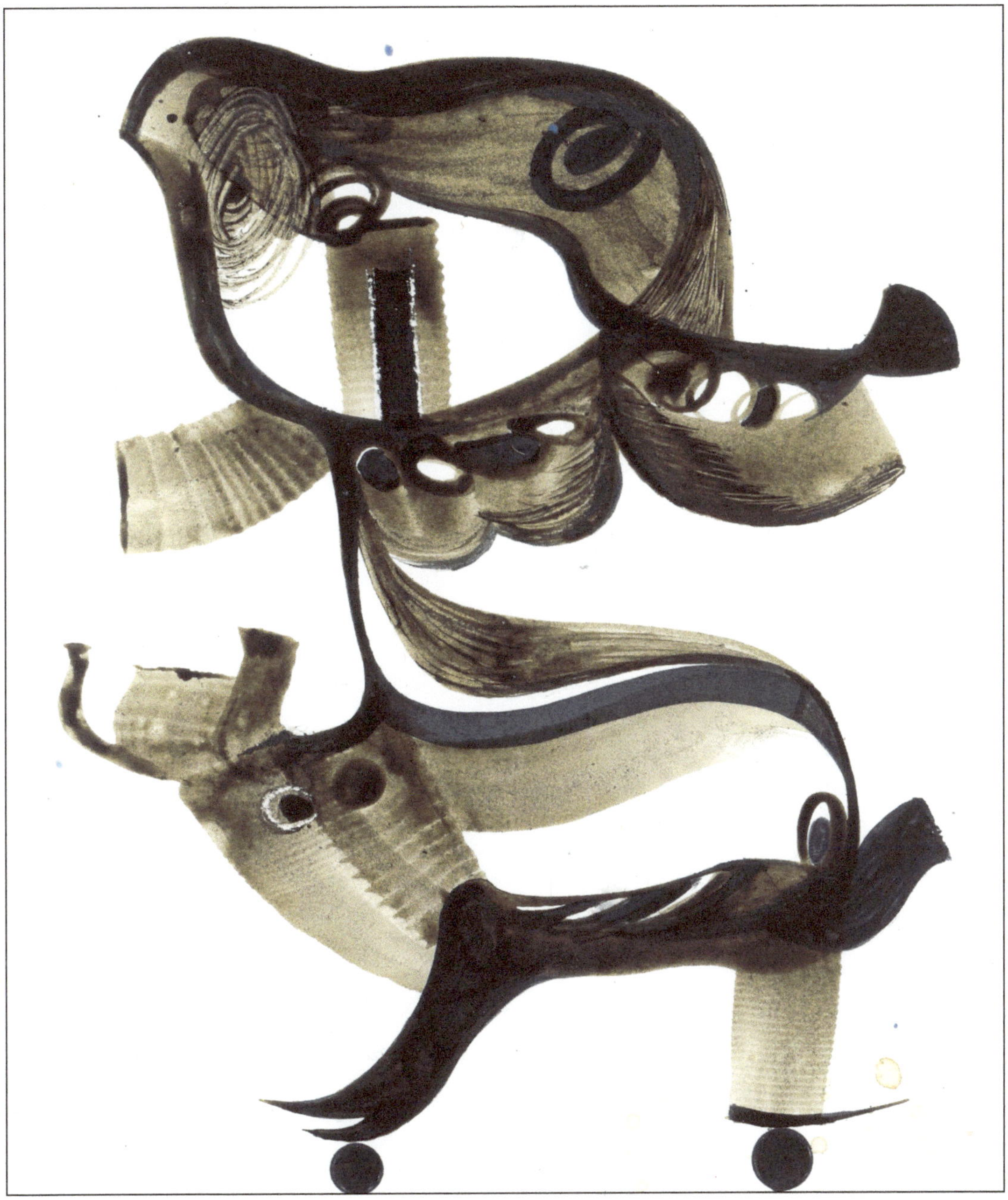

Eugene James Martin, untitled, s.d. (1982), 9.8 X 7"

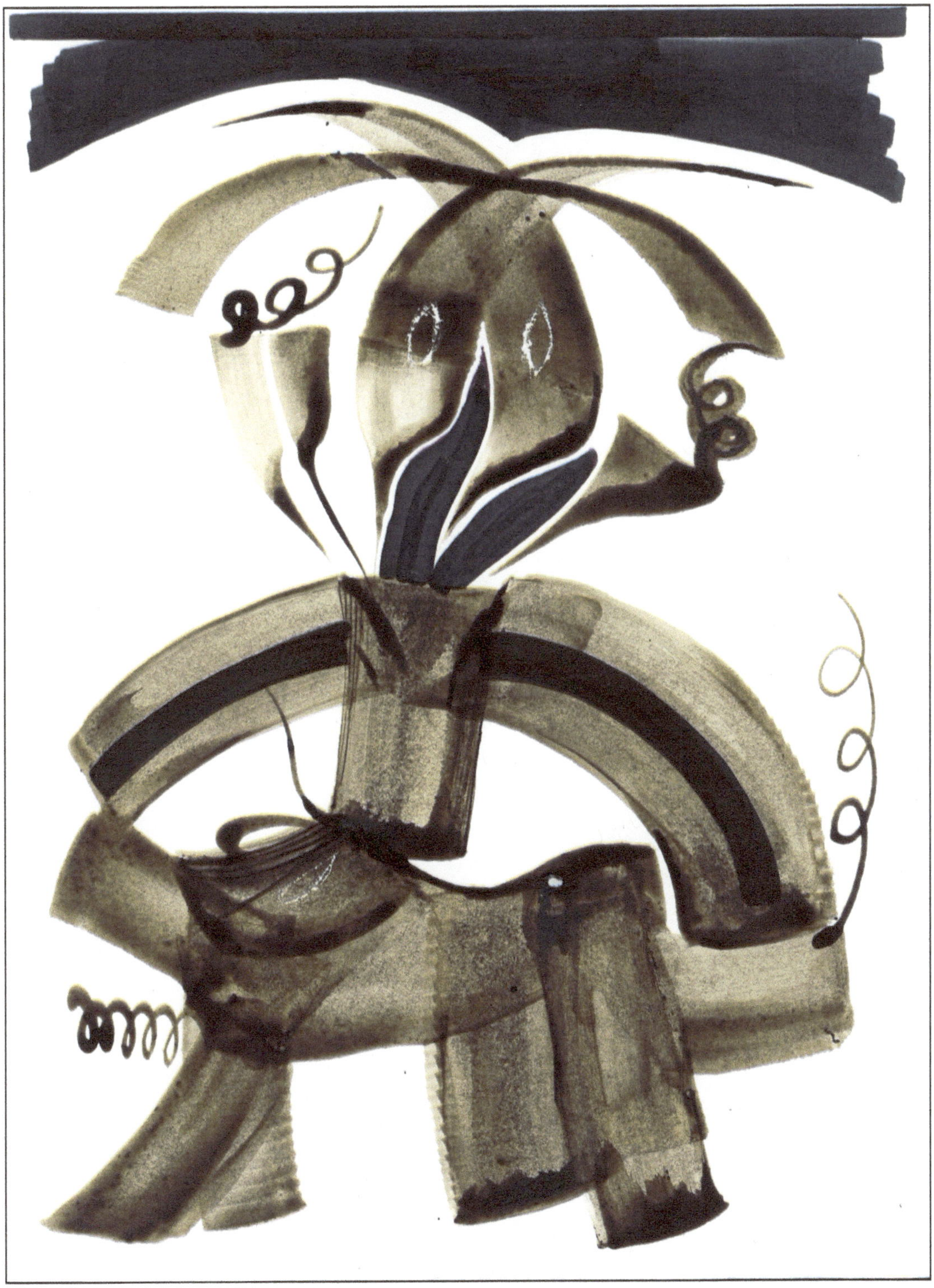

Eugene James Martin, untitled, 1982, 10 x 7.5"

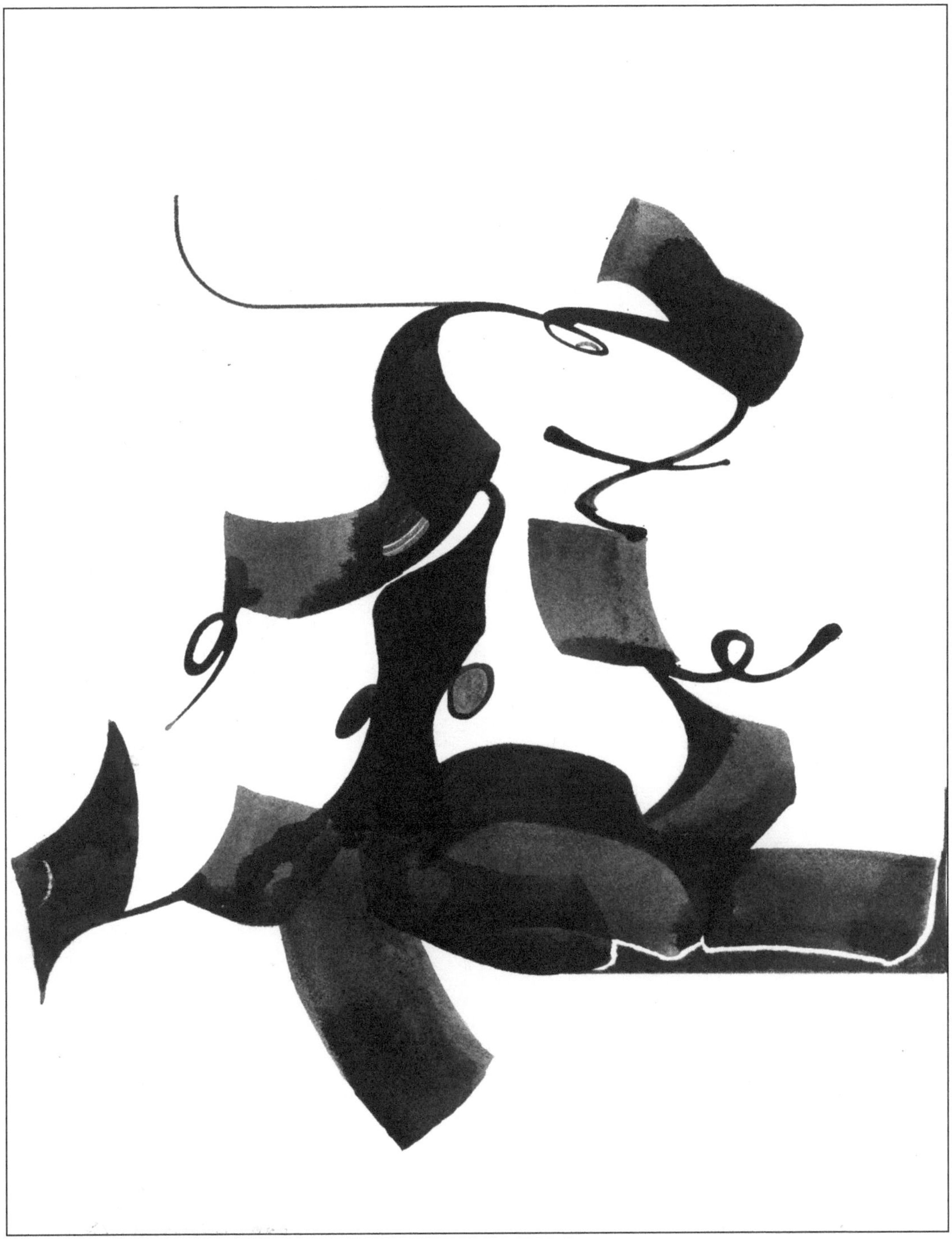

Eugene James Martin, untitled, 1982, 9 x 7"

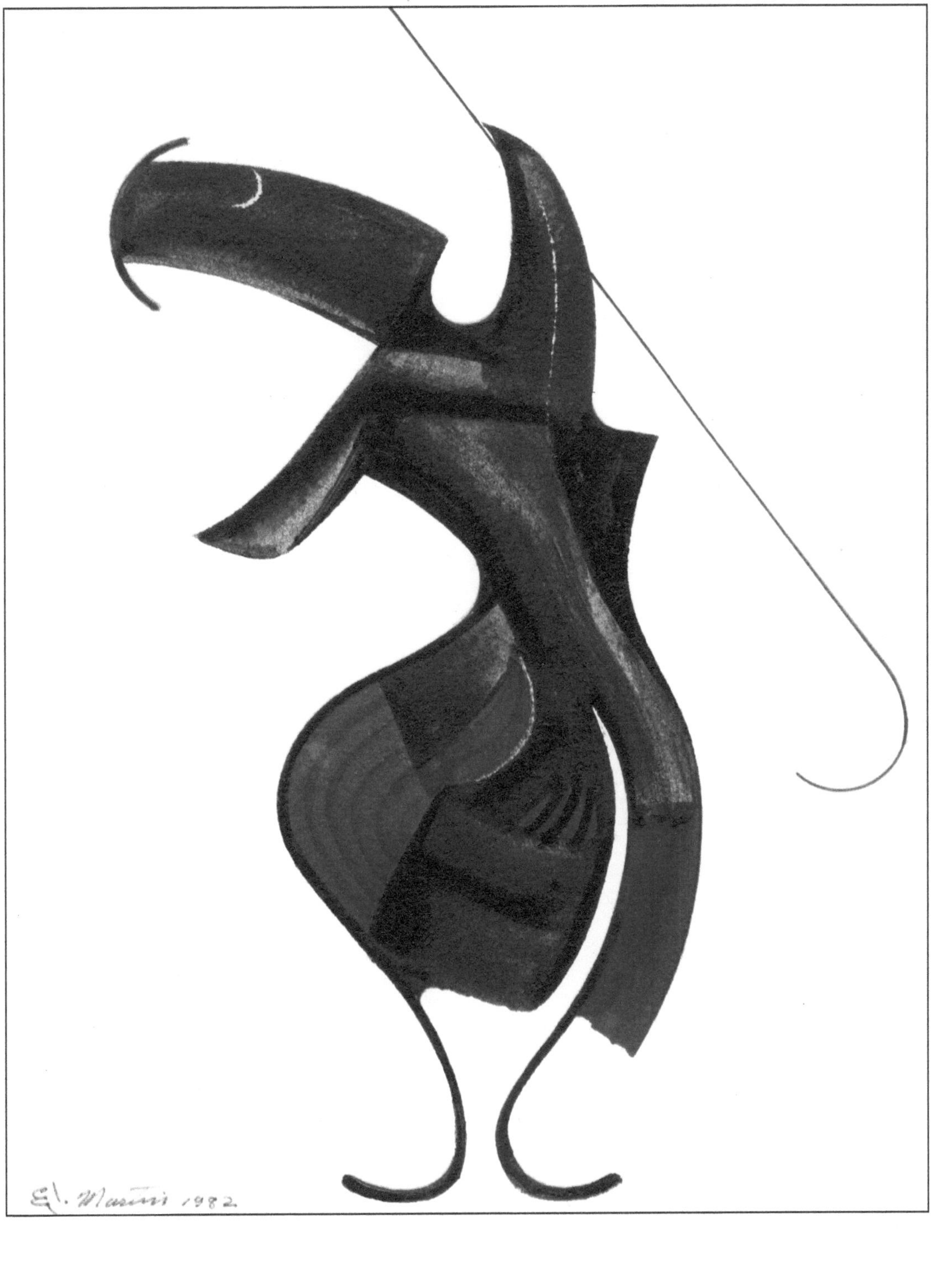
E.J. Martin 1982

Milton Keynes UK
Ingram Content Group UK Ltd.
UKHW050240241023
431212UK00002B/60

9780578028729